Stadium Stories:
New York Jets

D1521947

Stadium Stories™ Series

Stadium Stories:

New York Jets

Randy Lange

INSIDERS' GUIDE®

GUILFORD, CONNECTICUT
AN IMPRINT OF THE GLOBE PEQUOT PRESS

INSIDERS' GUIDE®

Text design: Casey Shain

Cover photos: *front cover:* Curtis Martin (Bill Kostroun/AP); *back cover:* top, Joe Namath (AP); bottom, fans (Peter Morgan/AP)

Library of Congress Cataloging-in-Publication Data is available.

ISBN 0-7627-3783-2

Manufactured in the United States of America
First Edition/First Printing

To the memory of Ray DeGraw, who helped me
keep my eye on the ball.

Contents

When Titans Roamed 1

The Era of Joe 15

Fireman Ed and Joey B 31

The New York Sack Exchange 45

A Thanksgiving of Pain 59

For Chrebet, the Fight Is Not Over 75

The Tuna Has Landed 91

Woebegone Ones, Terrible Twos 107

Curt's Determined Climb 127

International Arrival? 141

Acknowledgments

I couldn't have written this book without the help of the many knowledgeable and passionate people I've met over the years while covering my beat. Thank you to current Jets Herman Edwards, Chad Pennington, Wayne Chrebet, Curtis Martin, Jonathan Vilma, Ray Mickens, and Jon McGraw; former Jets Don Maynard, Marty Lyons, John Dockery, and Chad Cascadden; Walt Michaels from his Pennsylvania farm and Dick Haley from sunny, talent-laden Florida; and media relations associates Frank Ramos, Doug Miller, and Ron Colangelo. Knowing Joe Benigno and "Fireman" Ed Anzalone, I had to do a chapter on the fans who bleed Jets green. Thanks also to my compatriots in the mushroom cellar: Vinny "Sage" DiTrani, my good friend Dan Leberfeld, Rich Cimini, and Gerald Eskenazi, who knows more than I have time to ask. *Record* sports editor John Balkun insists I now start writing about "real sports," aka Major League Baseball. More thanks to Mary Norris, Mike Urban, and Jim Gigliotti for staying with me on this project. Finally, Rose, I couldn't have spent years frolicking in the toy department without your love and support.

Introduction

Quarterback Chad Pennington caused a tempest in the press-room late in the 2004 regular season when he chided beat reporters for not giving him and his New York Jets teammates enough credit for fighting their way to a ten-win season and an NFL playoff berth. "It is a privilege and an honor for me to play for the Jets," Pennington told the writers in front of television cameras and streaming audio on the Jets Web site. "And it should be a privilege and an honor for you to cover the Jets."

What a firestorm! First the columnists and writers weighed in, under such tabloid back-page hammerheads as "Chaddup!" and "Chad Melts Down." Pete Kendall, the Jets' well-read guard, watched the fallout and recalled something Mark Twain once said: "Never pick a fight with someone who buys ink by the barrel."

Then the fans responded. A good portion supported the newspapers, especially those schoolteachers, roofers, software salesmen, and sanitation workers who barely knew who Pennington was. "It's a pleasure to come to work today," they told each other with a Steve Martin-like lack of sincerity, from a cubicle or around the watercooler the rest of that week.

But another group also emerged, clearly in the quarterback's corner. "I make more than most of you beat writers," one e-mailer told me, "but I would give that up just to do the job you do. You don't know how lucky you are."

My view of the Sports Journalism 101 course that Pennington conducted was that he shouldn't have given that lecture. It wasn't a good public-relations move for him, and it was a really bad idea to antagonize all the newspapers in the New York area that the Jets had been wooing for months to support their plan to build a new pleasure-dome stadium on Manhattan's Lower West Side.

But I do know how lucky I am. On purely a personal level, I agree with Chad—I consider it a privilege to cover the Jets.

I've been reporting on pro football in the highly competitive New York market since 1979, and I have been a beat writer covering the Jets for *The Record* of Hackensack, New Jersey, and a frequent radio and TV contributor on Gang Green since 1994. I know, in talking with my audience and reading my e-mail, how important the NFL and the Jets are to people. The game is simultaneously elemental and complex, mundane and spectacular, played by men larger than life, yet for the most part down to earth. And I have a front-row seat for the entire show.

I've always said this is a great country, considering that athletes can make millions doing what they do and writers can make tens of thousands writing about it.

I haven't made any history in covering this great game for a quarter of a century, but it's been neat to have a small hand in rewriting history. For example, in 1995 the Jets' Ron Carpenter initially finished second in the NFL with a 26.3-yard kickoff-return average. However, I pointed out to the Elias Sports Bureau, the arbiter and keeper of pro football's statistics, that a scoring error might have been made because Carpenter muffed his last return of the season, but the ball was recovered by a teammate, which meant he shouldn't have been charged with a return for zero yards. When Elias reviewed the play and agreed, Carpenter's average was bumped up to 27.7—and past Glyn Milburn's 27.0 average for Denver and into first place.

In 1998 the Dolphins Dan Marino threw what initially was ruled a lateral to fullback Rob Konrad for a 4-yard rushing loss against the Jets. However, the "lateral" was going forward at the line of scrimmage, meaning it should have been a pass. So Marino (just elected to the Pro Football Hall of Fame in his first year of eligibility) has NFL career records of 8,358 passes and 4,967 completions that are each one more than they would have been, and a record of 61,361 yards that is 4 yards fewer than it would have been, had I not raised the question. (Marino likely doesn't care that his career passer rating of 86.38 with the pass is lower than the 86.39 it would have been without it.)

I did the reverse in 2001, inquiring about two plays scored as receptions by Curtis Martin. Both were changed to laterals— rushes—giving Martin 28 more rushing yards that he wouldn't have had in his quest to beat out Priest Holmes of the Chiefs for the NFL rushing title. (It didn't help; Martin still finished second, 42 yards behind Holmes's 1,555.)

Unfortunately, I still haven't found a scoring discrepancy to give the Jets their second Super Bowl victory to go with their tour de force in Super Bowl III so long ago.

But feeling honored and having fun doing a job doesn't alter the job I have to do. One of the most frequent questions I'm asked by Jets fans is: Are you a fan of the Jets? I can't be, not in the sense of the people I write about in this book (like Fireman Ed and Joey B). I'm not paid to root for the team but rather to fairly report on all its ups and downs over the course of a season. I developed a "rule of thirds" when I was the editor of an independent newspaper covering the football Giants in the eighties: roughly one-third of your audience thinks you're too easy on their team, one-third thinks you're too tough, and one-third likes whatever you do. Favor one-third over another only at your peril.

Yet being fair and balanced doesn't mean you can't be happy when good things happen to the good people you see virtually every day for six or seven months every year. Losing locker rooms provide the best stories, but winning locker rooms are good for the players and for my business.

The Jets have had a number of good guys who've finished last, third—indeed, every place but first—over the years since that glorious upset of the Colts. Being a good guy guarantees nothing, but being young, fast, and skilled helps a lot, and the 2005 Jets have all those traits. Perhaps a Super Bowl with this group is doable.

And if it happens, I plan on having the privilege of covering it.

When Titans Roamed

Don Maynard has always called El Paso home, but there's also a little home away from home, about 160 miles from El Paso in the mountains of New Mexico where he spends a lot of time. "I've been doing a project up here," he says, his West Texas twang still familiar to New York football fans of a certain age, "for twenty-two years."

The project is a ranch he has as part of a trust, and to this day he still gets his boots dirty as the spread's de facto engineer: damming a creek here, constructing a bridge there, raising a barn, hauling concrete. He hasn't let up, even though in January 2005, he celebrated his seventieth birthday.

Listen to Maynard as he takes a late-night break from his chores on a cold February night, condensation billowing from his mouth toward the twinkling stars of the Southwest, and reminisces about how this project has taken shape: "First you build a one-room house. Then the next three months, you build a garage so you've got a place inside to work. Then another room, then a kitchen—you expand, you keep building till you have six rooms. Then you put up a horse corral and your horse barn. At first you've got one stall, then two, then stalls for thirteen horses.

"Around the ranch you can see elk and deer running wild. Recently I counted sixteen turkeys running around, and nine ducks on a pond—I don't know how they keep from freezing—and a family of skunks down there, too. You just gradually keep leaning toward going back to the ranch more and more. It's just nice to come up here and enjoy the clean mountain air."

From this we can infer several things about Maynard. He has a fine attention for detail and numbers. He doesn't mind roughing it. And he loves a good adventure.

All these traits have been on display before, such as forty-five years ago when Maynard, then a young wide receiver who had played his college ball at the University of Texas–El Paso, and a band of brothers got together and lifted the New York Titans off the ground. That of course, is how the Jets spent the first three years of their existence in the fledgling American Football League, as Titans. And it can be argued that Maynard, at an unimpressive 6' and 180 pounds, was as huge a figure as anyone else for keeping the Titans viable enough to be purchased by Sonny Werblin's ownership group from New Jersey's Monmouth Park Racetrack in 1964, turned into the Jets, and launched toward Super Bowl III and beyond.

Harry Wismer certainly wasn't that figure. Wismer was the flamboyant, egomaniacal, wheeler-dealer first owner of the Titans—the only owner, in fact, unless you include the AFL itself in 1962. He gets credit for being there in the beginning, as one of the league's six original principal owners in 1959. But he was no Lamar Hunt, Barron Hilton, or K. S. "Bud" Adams Jr. (three other original AFL owners) in the financial department, and by 1962, his third year as owner, his business acumen had run the Titans into the ground.

As quarterback Lee Grosscup understated in his book, *Fourth and One*, about 1962, "It was a truly unusual season." Paychecks bounced, rumors flew that on a given day the players might not have a field to practice on, home crowds never bigger than 21,000 rattled around inside the hulking, decrepit Polo Grounds, and adjectives such as "chaotic" and "laughable" were being used daily in stories on the team. Finally Wismer went bankrupt, and commissioner Joe Foss and the AFL headquarters assumed the financial responsibility of running the Titans for the final five games of the season.

No, Wismer was not that historic figure.

Nor was Sammy Baugh, the former star quarterback, defensive back, and punter for the Washington Redskins, who did his best with the bad hand he was dealt trying to fashion the Titans into a winner in his two seasons as their first head coach. Baugh was universally loved by his players, but his wrangling with Wismer over money and personnel issues allowed him to say only that he never coached a nonlosing team in the AFL—the Titans went 7–7 both years before he faded from the picture, after a financial dispute with Wismer. (The year after the Titans died, Baugh was inducted into the Pro Football Hall of Fame.)

Nor were any of the Titans quarterbacks historically significant. Al Dorow, the journeyman from the NFL, did well in the Titans' first year in 1960, throwing 26 touchdowns and 26 interceptions—not a bad ratio for quarterbacks of the day—but then threw fewer touchdowns and more interceptions the next year and was gone. Grosscup and Johnny Green underwhelmed in 1962 and their careers, not just as Titans but as pro quarterbacks, were done.

Nor were any of New York's defenses, which, despite the presence of budding Pro Bowl linebacker Larry Grantham, gave up an average of almost four touchdowns a game over the Titans' forty-two-game life and got worse every year.

No, the general reason for the Titans' modest success was their offensive strategy. Several years later Joe Namath alluded to the difference between the offensive philosophies of the AFL and NFL, asking, "How many NFL teams have a quarterback who could complete as many passes to their wide receivers as we do? In our league we throw much more to our wide receivers than they do in theirs. I could've completed 80 percent if I dropped the ball off to my backs."

"It was a spread-type offense," Maynard recalled of Baugh's Titan-ic strategy. "It always tickles me when people write and talk about offenses today as if they were just invented. Bill Walsh, a super friend of mine, called it the West Coast offense, but he

Sammy Baugh, wearing hat and whistle, gets the Titans to break a sweat. AP

didn't do that until 1985. We were doing that with the Titans back in 1960. It was just normal football for us, but somebody got to add a little name to it."

That Maynard got to be involved out of the gate in fashioning the Titans' and later the Jets' high-octane offenses is a little piece of football serendipity. A 1957 ninth-round draft choice of the crosstown-rival New York Giants, he was cut by Allie Sherman after his rookie NFL season in 1959, then spent a season in the Canadian Football League before returning south of the border to the AFL.

He came back because he knew Sammy Baugh from playing against Baugh's Hardin-Simmons teams in the mid-fifties, and because Harry Wismer offered him a contract. But he put his full faith in this new enterprise because of Wismer's business partners.

"Two things guide my life, and those are common sense and reality, in any decision or discussion, whether it's politics or whatever," Maynard said. "With men like Lamar Hunt, Bud Adams, Barron Hilton, the guy in Buffalo [Ralph Wilson], I said, 'Gee whiz, here are successful men, well to do. Lamar Hunt could lose a million dollars a day for five years and it would never affect his budget in the league. He's going to make it go.'

"I was real optimistic. I knew I was going to get a fair chance with the Titans. I knew politics was not going to get me. And I was fortunate enough to sign a no-cut contract, so I knew I was going to stay for three years as far as the team was concerned. Then with ABC, that was the one television network that wasn't tied up. That's the thing we had going for us."

Naturally Maynard had a few things going for him on the field. One was blinding speed. Another, at least initially, was the tendency of opponents to underestimate him. Linebacker Bob Marques told Bill Ryczek in his book, *Crash of the Titans*, that he could still picture the nonconformist Maynard getting off the team bus for the first time. "A cowboy hat, dungarees, cowboy boots, and one of those big belt buckles. I thought, 'Who the hell is this guy?'" Marques said. "He was so skinny, I thought somebody was going to break him in half. That shows you how much I know."

Soon to become another plus for Maynard was Baugh's realization that he needed a pass-catching teammate, prompting the Titans to sign another CFL refugee in the 6'3", 211-pound Art

Powell. "We had a real good end in Don Maynard," Baugh said. "I was talking to Al Dorow before one of our first practices started and he asked me, 'If we can do just one thing to help our ball club, what would you say we needed?' And I said, 'We need a goddamn end opposite Maynard or they'll double-team him all the time. We need an end opposite him to keep them honest.' So we brought in Art Powell, who was a big, fast guy."

Some may argue that Powell was even more dynamic than Maynard. In their three seasons together, Powell wound up with more receptions (204 to 171), yards (3,178 to 2,935), and touchdowns (27 to 22).

One thing's for sure, the two of them together gave the Titans a one-two punch during their three troubled seasons. In fact they were the first wideout duo in AFL–NFL history to both finish with more than 1,000 yards in the same season, turning the trick in their very first season together, 1960. "Powell made a difference in our ball club," Baugh said. "When we got him, we had two damn good pass receivers."

Of course the Titans rarely had a damn good field to perform on, home or away. Their home field was the aforementioned Polo Grounds, once the venerable Harlem home of the baseball Yankees and Giants and the football Giants, which had become the best available option for the Titans and baseball's new New York franchise, the Mets.

"At the time it wasn't a good place to play," said Baugh, ever profanely, from his own ranch in Rotan, Texas. "The stands were dirty and everything. I never did like the place. It had the dirtiest goddamn stands. I don't know how they got anybody to buy tickets, to tell you the truth."

Maynard chose to see the relic of a stadium as a vessel half full. "At the Polo Grounds, there was a little bit of a low spot, a gully going across the field at an angle. That saved a couple of touchdowns and interceptions for us every year," he said, still punctuating observations that amuse him with a college boy's raspy chuckle after all these years. "And some fields were similar, and maybe the locker rooms and the showers weren't the best. At Buffalo one year, it got so cold we didn't shower after the game. The same thing happened in Kansas City."

In short, playing in the AFL was a rite of passage. "It was just like growing up as kids—we were poor but we just didn't know it," Maynard said. "We just went out and enjoyed life. We were glad to be there. And most of the fans who came out, they were glad to see us, too. That first year, I think the Titans scored more points than any other team in pro football. And that meant we were entertaining."

Maynard's memory for numbers remains sharp—the Titans indeed led all of pro football in 1960 with 382 points. It must be said, though, that Cleveland led the NFL with 362 points in a twelve-game schedule, giving the Browns the best per-game average at 30.2 compared with 27.3 for the Titans.

The highlights of that first season were the home-and-home games against Lamar Hunt's Dallas Texans. In the fourth game on the schedule, played at the Cotton Bowl, Dorow threw four touchdown passes (including one each to Maynard and Powell) and ran in a fifth score as the Titans outlasted the Texans 37–35. On Thanksgiving Day at the Polo Grounds, the Titans prevailed again 41–35, with Maynard and Powell again each grabbing one touchdown toss from Dorow.

Don Maynard's Career Receiving Statistics

Year		Number	Yards	Average	Touchdowns
1958	N.Y. Giants	5	84	16.8	0
1960	N.Y. Jets	72	1,265	17.6	6
1961	N.Y. Jets	43	629	14.6	8
1962	N.Y. Jets	56	1,041	18.6	8
1963	N.Y. Jets	38	780	20.5	9
1964	N.Y. Jets	46	847	18.4	8
1965	N.Y. Jets	68	1,218	17.9	14
1966	N.Y. Jets	48	840	17.5	5
1967	N.Y. Jets	71	1,434	20.2	10
1968	N.Y. Jets	57	1,297	22.8	10
1969	N.Y. Jets	47	938	20.0	6
1970	N.Y. Jets	31	525	16.9	0
1971	N.Y. Jets	21	408	19.4	2
1972	N.Y. Jets	29	510	17.6	2
1973	St. Louis	1	18	18.0	0
TOTALS		633	11,834	18.7	88

The season finished with one of those classic AFL shootouts that preceded the high-scoring affairs of another AFL, the Arena Football League, by three decades. It was a 50–43 loss to the Chargers, played in the Chargers' first home, the Los Angeles Coliseum, before they moved down I-5 to San Diego. Despite dropping them to 7–7, the loss gave the Titans and their cult of supporters some excitement for what was to come in 1961.

That excitement dissipated despite a 3–1 start that included home-and-home wins over the Boston Patriots and was gone when the season ended with another 7–7 thud. The last game that season, Maynard recalled, was in Dallas and came complete with a business flight from hell more appropriate for the over-crowded La Guardia Airport of the new millennium than the LGA of the sixties.

"We got to Dallas, but the weather was so cold and snowy and stuff that we had to turn around. Instead of landing at Oklahoma City or anywhere else down that way, we went all the way back to La Guardia," Maynard said. "The next morning, the day of the game, we woke up, got on the plane in the hangar, flew down again, and dressed on the airplane. Then when we landed, we rushed over to the stadium, put on our pads, and walked out on the field without really warming up that much."

The Texans predictably opened a 28–0 lead in the second quarter. The Titans unpredictably battled back to within 28–24 before falling 35–24.

The third season was as much a disaster on the field as in the front office. The Titans finished 5–9, losing four of their last five after Harry Wismer gave up the financial ghost. Their only win in that stretch was at least entertaining in the AFL fashion, a 46–45 victory over the Broncos at Denver, secured on Johnny Green's 3-yard touchdown toss to Art Powell.

In the off-season Sonny Werblin's group took over the Titans and rechristened them the Jets. The name was not in honor of the aircraft that notoriously fly over Shea Stadium these days, because Shea wasn't completed for business until 1964, but in reference to a new jet-setting modern era of New York football (and perhaps

Don Maynard brought sure hands and blinding speed to the Titans in 1960. AP

also because the name rhymed with Mets, the team they would share a contentious Shea relationship with in the coming years).

Frank Ramos, then the newly hired public relations director of the Jets, remembered opening up the file cabinets that the Titans left behind and finding the cupboard virtually bare. "There were two copies of the final AFL statistics from 1962 and a couple of AFL books, but the Titans never printed a media guide," Ramos said. "And in the photo files, there were maybe four or five pictures of Don Maynard, a couple of Larry Grantham, [halfback-punter] Curley Johnson, and [fullback] Bill Mathis—and about a hundred pictures of Harry Wismer."

The one asset the Jets kept and that appreciated through the Namath years and the Super Bowl season was Maynard himself (they let Powell go to the Oakland Raiders). Maynard is honest about his displeasure with such matters as the way Allie Sherman treated him and others with the Giants, his initial low salary, and how careerwise, after he retired following playing a spot role with the St. Louis Cardinals in 1973, he considered himself years behind his friends from high school and college and with a "Mickey Mouse pension" from the NFL.

But Maynard the builder expressed no regrets about constructing a Pro Football Hall of Fame career, studded with still-franchise records of 627 receptions, 11,732 yards, and 88 touchdowns, on that seemingly shaky American Football League foundation. "The best part of playing in the new league was that some of us wanted a second chance and the new league gave it to us," he said. "I always used to feel that Mets fans were really Yankees fans who couldn't get tickets, and maybe the Titans and Jets fans were really Giants fans who couldn't get tickets. Then all

Don Maynard stood on his head for some of his franchise-record 627 catches.
John Duricka/AP

of a sudden, the Jets started winning and they all claimed us. But it went all the way back to the Polo Grounds and those people who couldn't get into Giants games, so they came to us and found a few players they liked. It worked out great for me.

"I'm one of those guys who likes to see new types of businesses, new things going on," he said from the New Mexico high country. "We've got a lot of history, and I think there's a camaraderie there among the old AFL players that will never die."

The Era of Joe

Joe Namath and the Beatles have much in common. Broadway Joe got a later start, in the mid-sixties, but quickly proved able to whip his fans into Fab Four–like frenzies. In the ensuing years both entities aged like fine wine, to the point where at times they seemed forgotten, a long-ago passion only occasionally dusted off and admired by the true faithful . . . until they bubble back into the great American consciousness for a while, letting us know their respective eras still have not ended.

For Namath that notion was underscored in 2003 when Woody Johnson, the natty, trim Uber-fan owner of the New York Jets, strutted around practice in business suit and tie—and the special baseball cap, all green except for the simple white numbers "1" and "2" on the front.

"It's in honor of Joe's sixtieth birthday and in honor of what he did for the Jets," said Johnson, the club's owner since 2001. "In many respects he's the most important player in the history of the franchise."

Flash forward to Super Bowl XXXIX in February 2005. Days before Paul McCartney delivered a crowd-pleasing trip down memory lane with a lavish halftime set that included three songs from his Beatles incarnation, Joe Willie's name was invoked again. It was during the mind-numbing series of interviews of the New England Patriots and Philadelphia Eagles in the days before the big game when wide receiver Freddie Mitchell, one of the Eagles' mouths that roared, was asked if he'd guarantee a victory over the Patriots. "I'm not Joe Namath," Mitchell said with a scowl.

Mitchell was, of course, referencing Namath from thirty-six years before, when he was the shaggy-haired counterculture superstar with the number 12 on his back, the hair-trigger release, and monster arm, and he issued The Guarantee that the Jets would beat the 17- , 18- , even 19-point-favorite Baltimore Colts in Super Bowl III—then backed it up by orchestrating the 16–7 upset. Even in the new millennium, it wouldn't be a Super Bowl if some players and coaches weren't asked if they have similar guarantees in them. And they never do, because Namath had been there and done that way back on January 9, 1969, at the Miami Touchdown Club.

As Namath once said at poolside at the Galt Ocean Mile Hotel in Fort Lauderdale, the Jets' Super Bowl III hotel, "This wasn't the way I planned it." He was talking about the furor of that particular Hype Week but could have been offering self-commentary from the middle of his storied run as an American idol.

Joseph William Namath first appeared on pro football's radar screen as the hotshot Alabama quarterback labeled by the iconic Bear Bryant as "the greatest athlete I've ever coached." He was a

The Jets rode Joe Namath's vision all the way to victory in Super Bowl III. AP

superb passer, naturally, with one of the all-time quickest releases and biggest arms in the game. He still holds Jets records for most pass attempts in a career (3,655); most yards in a game (496 against Baltimore in 1972), season (4,007 in 1967), and career (27,057); and most touchdown passes in a game (6 versus the Colts in 1972) and career (170). "He could throw a ball through a wall," said John Schmitt, his center for nine seasons.

But Namath, at first, was also a dangerous runner with a nose for the end zone. He ran for 15 touchdowns with the Crimson Tide and 7 in his twelve-year career as a Jet, including two in one game against Oakland in 1966. No Jets quarterback had duplicated that feat until Chad Pennington dashed for two scores against New England in 2003.

He also had an uncanny intelligence at deciphering defenses, admittedly much simpler than today's Xs and Os. And contrary to his public image, at practice he was a hard-working lunch-pail guy from Beaver Falls, Pennsylvania. "Joe was as plain as any of the rest of us. That's the way we accepted him, that's the way it was," said wide receiver Don Maynard, who was thirty years old and a six-year pro when Namath, not quite twenty-two, signed that renowned $427,000 rookie contract to spurn the NFL (the St. Louis Cardinals selected him twelfth overall in the established league's draft) and join the Jets in 1965.

"I know as a rookie he came in and got that big bonus. But he came out early, stayed late, did the things that would make him what he wanted to be, the same as the rest of us," Maynard said. "He paid the price. He worked just as hard and studied as much film as anybody else. In that way, naturally, you accept the guy by the things he does. He comes to play and he comes to win."

Besides his physical skills and his winning way, Namath also clearly was refining that rebel attitude, that sense of timing and style that augmented and transcended the NFL and sports. He wore mink off the field, white shoes on it. He grew his hair long, not only on his head but also on his Fu Manchued face. He always partied like it was 1999, as captured in one of his favorite sayings: "I like my women blonde and my Johnnie Walker Red."

All of these were lightning rods for an American culture in the process of redefining itself. As a result, Namath entered the Jets' Super Bowl season possessing the aura of white-hot celebrity. Like something out of *A Hard Day's Night*, he hid in equipment trucks and laundry bins to get past throngs of fans and meet the team buses down the road on the way to flights back from road games.

And when Namath dropped back to pass, the possibilities were endless. "I had no idea how important a figure Joe was," said Gerald Eskenazi, the venerable *New York Times* beat writer and author of *Gang Green*, "until I actually went to games and saw the whole stadium stand up the first time he went into his backpedal. There was such anticipation at what was about to happen."

Helping grow the Namath legend was the almost vagabond nature of the Jets in the sixties. Because of their second-class status behind the Mets in the teams' Shea Stadium leases, they would not only open most regular seasons with long stretches of road games while the Mets finished up their schedule, but they would also tour the country for their "home" preseason games, stopping in such venues as Alexandria (Virginia), Birmingham (Alabama), Jacksonville (Florida), Cincinnati (Ohio), and Memphis (Tennessee). It was as if the circus had just pulled into town, and Joe Willie was the ringmaster.

It all culminated in Super Bowl III. First the Jets put together their 11–3 season, still the finest in their history. Then they had to beat back the challenge of the big, bad Raiders in the AFL title game, which they did—Namath, despite sustaining a second-quarter concussion, rallied them from a 23–20 fourth-quarter deficit with a long pass and a short touchdown toss to Don Maynard for the 27–23 win.

Then came Miami—Namath's friendly late-night (early morning) chat with Colts kicker Lou Michaels in Jimmy Fazio's restaurant, Namath holding court by the pool . . . The Guarantee.

Namath at first didn't want to go to the Miami Touchdown Club's awards dinner. "The players are having a barbecue that night," Namath told public relations director Frank Ramos (who would serve in that capacity from 1963, the franchise's first year as the Jets, through 2001, Herman Edwards's first as head coach). "I want to be with my teammates. Why should I be doing this event?"

Ramos convinced him to go, so Namath went unescorted to the dinner. After being heckled by several Baltimore fans with taunts like: "The Colts are gonna kick your ass!" he made his famous remarks.

"I think we'll win it. In fact I'll guarantee it." Or so he was quoted in *The Sports Encyclopedia*. But the *1969 American Football League Guide* has Joe saying: "Matter of fact, I think we'll win it. I'll GUARANTEE it." And then there is this version of the

Joe Namath hands off to Matt Snell, who helped lead the Jets past the Colts. AP

quote in Stephen Hanks's *The Game That Changed Pro Football*: "And we're going to win Sunday, I'll guarantee you."

The last version is how Namath remembers saying it. "The statement wasn't planned," Namath told Hanks twenty years later. "There wasn't a motive behind it. It was just something that needed to be said and was a spur-of-the-moment thing triggered by a loudmouth Colts fan at that dinner. When I look back at that period now, I realize not only was I a very confident young man, I was also very angry, actually. It was more or less anger and frustration stemming from how everybody was putting the team and the league down that led me to make that guarantee."

Reactions to The Guarantee ran the gamut. The Colts, predictably, were livid. And Jets coach Weeb Ewbank, at the team breakfast the next morning, has been described as if he'd just seen a ghost or lost half his family in some bizarre accident. "We can't be doing this," Ewbank spit out angrily to his team, "talking like this and giving them fuel."

Some of Namath's teammates were equally worried. "This guy is crazy," linebacker Ralph Baker remembered thinking. But others, as Ewbank spoke, exchanged jokes and smirks, as if to say, "Who cares if he guaranteed it? We know we're better than Baltimore."

In a way the episode may have galvanized the Jets for the game ahead. They saw in their quarterback more than a carousing playboy loose in New York City. After all, they voted him offensive captain for the first time at the beginning of the 1968 season. They wanted a leader, they chose him, and he was showing them the way.

"Joe's guarantee?" recalled John Schmitt, Namath's center. "We all said at the time, 'We'd better win, because Joe said so.'"

Added fullback Matt Snell: "We were just glad Joe didn't go any further and say, 'I guarantee we'll win . . . if they play the zone they've been playing all year.'"

John Dockery was a former Red Sox minor-leaguer for whom the Super Bowl would be his fifth game as an AFL rookie defensive back—he thanks Speedy Duncan's 95-yard punt return for the Chargers in game 11 for getting him promoted from the Jets' taxi squad. Dockery recalled how all the pregame hoopla converged as the team buses approached the Orange Bowl in the hours before the game. "All of a sudden, the buses were engulfed by fans," Dockery said. "It was a sea of humanity, and it started rocking our bus. I thought, 'They're going to turn this thing over. We're not going to make it.'

"It was because of Joe, of us being the underdogs from New York. And it was because of the times, all the young people so aligned with the Jets. We were these antiestablishment upstarts against the established NFL. We were a voice for the people, an image for the people, and Joe took that on. These young fans were just excited and cheering on a guy who was representing their vision."

Arguably, Namath's MVP vision in that game—along with his crisp passing, 17 for 28 for 206 yards, especially his eight hookups with George Sauer Jr. for 133 yards working against the Colts' bread-and-butter rotating strongside zone to which Snell had referred—was the high-water mark of his pro football career. The following season brought one of his low points, the 13–6 playoff loss to the Kansas City Chiefs in cold, windy Shea Stadium, when he completed 14 of 40 passes and threw 3 interceptions.

Namath by the Numbers

Here are some of the numbers that show quarterback Joe Namath's lasting influence:

1—Seasons Namath was in the *ABC Monday Night Football* booth. He teamed with Frank Gifford and O. J. Simpson in 1985. Perhaps most memorably, Joe was always known for pronouncing the word *play* with two syllables—"puh-LAY."

2—Guest appearances he has made on *The Simpsons*, in 1997 and 2002, the most recent of many gigs in a television entertainment career that he got rolling with appearances on *Rowan & Martin's Laugh-In* in 1971–72 and the *Tonight Show* appearances with Johnny Carson.

6—Theatrical-release motion pictures he's appeared in. The first was *Norwood* with Glen Campbell in 1970, playing a character named Joe William Reese. The others: *C. C. and Company* with Ann-Margret, 1971 (C. C. Ryder); *The Last Rebel*, 1971 (Burnside Hollis); *Avalanche* Express, 1979 (Leroy); *Chattanooga Choo Choo*, 1986 (Newt Newton); and *Going Under*, 1991 (Capt. Joe Namath).

9—Number of episodes taped in Joe's sitcom adventure, *The Waverly Wonders*, only four of which aired in September–October 1978. He played Joe Casey, a washed-up pro basketball player turned history teacher and hoops coach at Waverly High in Wisconsin.

208—Number of individuals on President Richard Nixon's "enemies list" of 1971. Namath was one of ten celebrities and the only athlete to make the list.

300—Number of "sexual conquests" Joe estimated he'd had over the years in a 1969 *Playboy* interview.

1973—The year he made a TV commercial wearing a pair of Hanes Beautymist pantyhose (not L'Eggs, as some recall). He knew the spot would be controversial, but he said, "Let's do it. I can take the heat."

10,000—Amount of dollars Namath received from Schick for shaving off his Fu Manchu mustache in a 1974 television commercial.

Joe Namath shares a chuckle with host Dick Martin before a taping of Laugh-In.
Nick Ut/AP

And the injuries began coming in bunches—broken wrist in 1970, torn knee ligaments in the first preseason game of 1971, shoulder separation in 1973. The 1972 season was at least Namathian: He channeled Broadway Joe in game 2 at Baltimore in his 496-yard, 6-touchdown performance in the 44–34 triumph and played almost the whole season. But the Jets couldn't rise above 7–7.

Even though the Jets 1976 media guide saw it differently, describing Namath, before his last season in green, as "the undisputed leader of the Jets' offense," the truth was something else. "When I started covering the team, Joe was a legend and the team was already in its long decline," Gerry Eskenazi said. "It was like he was this historic figure in the locker room that everybody on the team was in awe of, and yet he wasn't any good anymore."

As a pro quarterback, at least. However, while Namath left the NFL not with a bang but with a whimper, he never completely left the New York or American psyche. He wasn't everywhere, but he kept popping up at odd moments to remind us he and his craggy good looks were still around to entertain us: bar owner Joe, talking head Joe, sitcom Joe, animated Joe.

Namath's calendar these days is crammed with national appearances for the Arthritis Huddle and with chairing the annual March of Dimes Walkathon in New York. He also has talked publicly about the depression he felt after his 1999 divorce, and to this day he continues to work at improving his family situation.

In his travels he still drops in and lends the Jets a hand. Woody Johnson's management team, aware of his impact on its

A more mature Joe Namath in front of his favorite street in his favorite city.

Tina Fineberg/AP

fan base, brought him back as a team spokesperson of sorts. Even current quarterback Chad Pennington has noted how Namath helped him at an autograph show. "I was signing my name, and you really couldn't read the 'Chad,'" Pennington said. "He told me, 'Look, you need to let them see your name. That's the most important thing in an autograph. Take time to spell your name out.' So I do that now—although I still have to fudge the 'Pennington' because it's a little too long."

One thing Namath isn't doing is contributing to others' books. He declined to cooperate on Mark Kriegel's 450-page biography, *Namath*, which was published last year. "Joe didn't agree to participate in the book, and he wasn't that happy with the book," a friend said. "There was a lot of stuff that was in the book that was true, but that didn't need to be brought up again."

Yet Namath is only semireclusive. He continues to do television interviews, including the one he shouldn't have done, when he twice told ESPN's Suzy Kolber during a live sideline interview, "I want to kiss you." Afterward he admitted he'd had too much to drink at a pregame reception and immediately entered alcohol rehab.

But there are no Simon Cowell insults for this American idol. We still want to kiss you, Joe, for what you've meant to us through the years. John Dockery, who's developed into a solid broadcaster and sideline reporter for CBS Radio and Westwood One, summed up the alchemy that turned Namath from golden boy on the field into a still-magnetic celebrity off it.

"Some people have that rare commodity that makes them a star that just glitters and shines. Joe had that quality. He was like Muhammad Ali and Joe DiMaggio, a cut above," Dockery said.

"And what's so special is that to be the best or among the best for one moment is very, very rare and special. The Jets were underdogs, they were ridiculed, but they had their moment in the sunshine. They were at the top of the mountain, the best of the best. Those are fond memories for Joe and fond memories for me."

Not to mention the rest of us who still like the idea that the Namath era has yet to end.

Fireman Ed and Joey B

Every pro sports franchise has a fan base
formed by unique circumstances. Still, Jets
fans have come out of a different crucible.
They began life as Giants followers shut out
of tickets and looking for a team they could
watch and love. Or they were youngsters
seeking a new, high-powered thrill after
becoming bored with the stodgy NFL. Or
they were Long Island natives surprised to

wake up in 1964 and find a pro football team playing in their backyards.

They struck it rich as the Titans became the Jets, who became champions of football in 1969, but they've been hitting dry wells ever since. And the experience has left them on many occasions a sarcastic, rowdy bunch. "A lot of teams have had it worse," says long-suffering Jets fan Joe Benigno after wrapping up his talk show on WFAN-AM in Queens, the borough the Jets called home for two decades. "Cleveland's never been to a Super Bowl. The Lions, the Saints, the Cardinals—teams have had worse histories. But Jets fans, we're still not the number-one team even in our area. We're still second fiddle to the Giants, although I see that gap closing.

"Now guys are growing up as Jets fans. Maybe they started in the early eighties—they've gone through twenty years of heartache. A guy who started in '72, '73, he's looking at thirty years. They're all starting to say, 'When am I going to see it?'"

Eddie Anzalone is one of those fans. See if you recognize Eddie's story. See if you recognize Eddie.

"I became a Jets fan in 1976, when I was fifteen years old," he recalls. "At that time I lived in College Point [New York] and was still playing high school football, and my brother Frank bought Jets season tickets. I remember playing in a game, then running home, giving my father my equipment, then running down College Point Boulevard and over the Flushing Bay Bridge to go to Shea Stadium to see the Jets play for the first time."

It wasn't long before the Jets relocated across the Hudson River, to the New Jersey Meadowlands. Anzalone didn't like the venue, in large part because of the name—Giants Stadium—but also because the stadium just didn't shake, rattle, and roll the way Shea did.

"My first year, 1984, my brother and I were in the lower tier, and it was dead there," he said. "My second year, I'm twenty-five, I'm a lunatic, and I'm running up and down the aisles trying to get the crowd going. Maybe 1,000 people would chant with me periodically. Then I go down to the front-row railing to let them see me and I almost fall over onto the field. My brother grabs me and says, 'Get on my shoulders.' I did, and we'd get 5,000 or 10,000 to chant with us on and off during the lean years."

You may have guessed by now that Anzalone is Fireman Ed, so christened by Chris Berman, ESPN's bestower of funky nicknames and a longtime Jets fan himself. Yes, Anzalone actually is a fireman with Engine 69 and Ladder 28 in Manhattan — "the Harlem Hilton," he says. Resplendent in white fire helmet and jersey number 42 in honor of former Jets spark plug Bruce Harper, he climbs onto the shoulders of a younger guy named Bruce who sits in front of him ("Frank's knees are shot," Ed says) and leads the crowd through that often mocked but rarely matched chant: "J-E-T-S, JETS-JETS-JETS!"

Anzalone recalls the story of the chant's Shea origins, which demonstrates the crude attitude possessed even by early Gang Green supporters. "When Baltimore used to come to town, this Colts fan used to run around the portable stands by the scoreboard, where the Colts fans used to sit. He'd go down there with a megaphone and lead the fans in 'C-O-L-T-S, COLTS-COLTS-COLTS!'" Ed says.

"A guy by the name of Larry Mack was a New York City fireman, Lieutenant's Engine 50 in the South Bronx. He was in the

"Fireman Ed" Anzalone is the number one cheerleader for today's Jets fans.
Bill Kostroun/AP

upper deck and he used to wear a colored wig. When Larry heard that chant, he decided he was going to do a Jets chant. 'Four letters are better than five,' he said. He had the letters *J* and *E* painted on his left buttock and *T* and *S* painted on his right buttock. Then he'd moon the opposing team and lead the chant from the upper deck."

Fireman Ed is the current caretaker of this cheeky ritual. He exposes only his stern visage, as much clenched fist as face, and leads the Meadowlands crowd several times a game in this simple and yes, inspirational cheer. "You've got to remember, we're the only team in all of professional sports with its own chant," Anzalone says. "Yeah, now you're hearing Eagles fans going, 'E-A-G-L-E-S,' but you don't hear the whole crowd doing it, and they got it from us anyway."

Anzalone's cheerleading has gotten him promoted to one of the faces of the Jets of the new millennium. His mug is on the DiamondVision scoreboards as he leads the fans in "J-E-T-S" or "DEE-FENSE." He can be spotted on NFL Films features on the Jets. He's even featured in a television spot trying to convince New Yorkers of the merits of a new stadium for the Jets on the West Side of Manhattan.

It's all been made possible because of Anzalone's long nurturing of the chant. As one football observer, unaware of Fireman Ed's power, said on seeing and hearing the cheer: "It's amazing. Fans are making all kinds of sounds, then one guy stands up and everybody gets quiet and he starts moving his arms, forming letters, and a whole stadium spells out the team's name as one."

"Really, it's an honor. I'm more humbled by it than anything," Ed says. "I don't feel superior. But do I feel I can make a difference? Yeah, I do. Seventy-six thousand fans give me the opportunity each week to get something done, to make it a home-field advantage for our team."

If Fireman Ed has become the face of Jets fandom, Joe Benigno is its voice. Benigno is a lifelong North Jerseyan who was a food salesman serving Manhattan and Brooklyn restaurateurs—until he got his dream job, as ESPN would label it, talking about sports and getting paid for it. For more than nine years, beginning Labor Day 1995, Benigno was the overnight host on WFAN Radio in New York.

Benigno, seven years older than Anzalone, actually traces his Gang Green roots back to Joe Namath's last season at Alabama, when his father, Joe Sr., counseled him, "You gotta watch this guy play" in the 1965 Orange Bowl. Joe listened to his pop and was hooked on number 12, which is why he became a Jets fan a few months later when they made Namath their first-round pick, and why, four years later, he had no doubt the Jets would beat the 17½-point-favorite Colts in Super Bowl III.

"My dad died in 1967, and I switched schools to Paramus [New Jersey] High School," Benigno reminisced. "I was a sophomore that year, and everybody in school was saying, 'The Jets have no shot; they have no way of winning this game.' Even though they were a New York team, most of the kids into football were still into the NFL. There weren't a lot of big-time Jets fans like me.

"I started taking bets on the game. I wasn't even getting any points. I was talking even money, and I took $200 worth of bets that we would win this game. And I remember the day before the game thinking, 'How am I getting the money to pay these guys off?' But I didn't have to, and I walked in the day after the game as king of the world. Guys are just throwing money at me and walking away. One guy hands me a bag—it was $10 in pennies. It was almost like that game gave me respect in that school from then on."

It's hard to say whether Benigno is less tortured because he at least got to witness a Super Bowl–winning Jets team or more so because he knows what he and his fellow fans are missing. Suffice to say, he has endured the ensuing three-plus decades with an increasingly bitter taste in his mouth.

The 1969 home playoff game against Kansas City, with the Jets as defending pro football champions, was a chilly 13–6 flop. "That's the game that gets lost in all of Jets history," he said. "I went to that game, sat in the end zone freezing. Namath was never the same after that game. And little did I know thirty-six years later I'd be sitting here still not having gotten back to the Super Bowl."

The seventies, he said, "were horrible. They didn't have one winning season."

The eighties featured the '81 team, which lost a home playoff game to the Bills; the '82 strike team, which lost the AFC Championship Game at Miami; and the '86 team, which limped into the playoffs after a 10–1 start but was in position in Cleveland to again advance to the conference title game—until Mark Gastineau's late hit turned a third and 24 into a touchdown drive that led the Browns back from a 10-point deficit to a 23–20 double-overtime comeback.

The nineties were ugly until Bill Parcells arrived in town. His first season, 1997, went well until the regular-season finale at Detroit, when, facing the prospect of win and get in, lose and go home, Parcells inexplicably took the ball out of quarterback Neil O'Donnell's hands on several occasions and the Jets lost, 13–10. The next season the Jets were poised again to go to the Super Bowl, with a 10–0 lead and twenty-six-plus minutes to play at Denver, before John Elway rescued the Broncos and again sank the Jets.

With the Herman Edwards era came two playoff losses at Oakland and then the debacle in Pittsburgh after the 2004–05 season, when Doug Brien missed tough field goals from 47 and 43 yards in the final two minutes of regulation, and the Steelers sneaked away with a 20–17 overtime present. "Nothing was worse than Gastineau [in 1986]," Benigno lamented, "until the Pittsburgh game."

The Jets aren't the only unrequited love of Benigno's life. He also bleeds for the Mets, Knicks, and Rangers from his bully pulpit, which has moved from overnights on WFAN to a midday teamup with Sid Rosenberg. "I think it's Benigno," Joe says, using the athletic third person to describe why his teams have struggled for so long. "Sometimes I say I don't live right. The teams I root for, it's amazing I'm alive. I really believe I'll never see the Jets win another Super Bowl in my lifetime. And the day I drop dead, I guarantee you they'll win it the next year."

Anzalone and Benigno are two of the most visible Gang Green fans, but there are millions lined up behind them. Some are celebrities in their own right, such as actors Adam Sandler and Kevin James and comedian Richard Jeni. These fans have teamed up to sell out Giants Stadium for every home game since 1989, a streak that has reached more than 130 games through 2004. And all those fans seem to come with a hidden edge. Win and things are fine, of course, but lose and out comes defeatism, cynicism, anger, and depression. One writer characterized Jets' fans as the football equivalent of Boston Red Sox fans (but that analogy no longer applies after the 2004 World Series).

These personality traits don't get any better when shaken and stirred with alcohol. One team newspaper ran a weekly feature called "Ask the Fans," for which opinions were solicited from

Highly Recommended

Joe Benigno's passion for football has impressed no less than Bill Belichick, who as the defensive coordinator for the Jets in the late nineties used to hop on the treadmill at five in the morning and while away the miles listening to Benigno do the last segment of his overnight shift before Don Imus and his crew took over the studio.

"I love Joe's perspective on football," Belichick said in 2004, before he guided the Patriots to their third Super Bowl championship in four seasons. "I think he's very knowledgeable, but he's also a great fan and a loyal supporter of his team. I have a lot of respect for his love as a fan, but also for his knowledge as somebody who follows sports, not particularly football. I don't know much about other sports like he does, but I know just a little bit about football. Joe is pretty perceptive and he's really into it. I enjoy that. I enjoy talking to him. And I have a tremendous respect for what he does."

That's quite a recommendation for Benigno's résumé.

spectators in the Meadowlands parking lots after games. The state of the fans was almost uniformly one of inebriation, leading the editor to consider renaming the feature "Ask the Drunks." And who can forget the 1988 Monday night game at Giants Stadium, when, either in a quest for warmth or a defiant act late in the 37–14 loss to the Bills, a small group set fire to a section of upper-tier end-zone stands?

Jets fans can be melodramatic, some are barely sane, and all are a breed apart.
Peter Morgan/AP

The rabid nature of the Jets fans is on display annually on the first day of the NFL draft. The league has always catered to its draftniks, at first by opening up small-capacity hotel balconies around the ballroom floor where the draft was taking place, then by moving the festivities to an annex in Madison Square Garden where more fans can be accommodated.

The Jets followers dominate this venue with the expressed intention of passing instant judgment on the team's first-round draft pick. "It's a special day for them," says Dan Leberfeld, who has run the independent newspaper *Jets Confidential* for a while. "Since they haven't been to the Super Bowl in thirty-five years, this is their Super Bowl. It's like Christmas to them. It's very melodramatic up there. The Jets' draft picks need instant therapy once commissioner Paul Tagliabue announces their names."

Tight end Kyle Brady was taken ninth overall by the Jets in the 1995 draft and jeered. "Oh, they're tough," Brady said with amazement. "I've never been booed before in my life. I'll have to go up there and make some friends."

Seven years later, defensive end Bryan Thomas was tabbed twenty-second overall (in 2002) and heckled. "I take that as motivation," the Alabama-Birmingham product said, somewhat tentatively. "You see people say 'Boo! Boo!' What they're saying is, 'We want a pick we know about and we've seen on TV.' I understand that. The people in New York haven't seen me perform. That's what I'm looking forward to, and it's just a lot of motivation for me."

This all makes Jets fans sound like a large group of soccer hooligans, but the portrait isn't complete. They are tough, but they are also fair. They have an edge, but it's just protection against the next difficult defeat. They are hard to please, but they can be pleased.

Doug Miller, the team's director of media relations, remembers the 1996 draft, when he arrived early at the Marriott Marquis Hotel in New York and saw a line of draftniks 3 city blocks long chanting "Keyshawn! Keyshawn!" then cheering wildly when the Jets indeed made wide receiver Keyshawn Johnson the first overall pick.

And defensive tackle Dewayne Robertson recalled the reaction he got when he was the fourth pick in 2003: "It was great. I heard stories that the fans might boo you, but I guess they liked me. They kind of went crazy when my name was called."

Herman Edwards may not like it when the fans occasionally sit on their hands, and he has come to despise the phrase "Same

A Meadowlands maestro, Fireman Ed gestures for the crowd to pump up the jam.
Dick Druckman/AP

old Jets" when reporters and fans throw it out as the catchall reason for the latest Gang Green meltdown. But he leaves no doubts
about how much he values a rocking stadium, such as in 2004
when the Jets won their first four home games. "The fans have
been great," Coach Herm said. "They're very supportive, vocal,
and loud. They're going to be loud. And they're smart. They
know when to holler and not to holler. Fireman Ed does a good
job getting them fired up, especially against the teams that aren't
in your division—that can be a really big factor for you. If we
keep winning, they'll stay excited."

That, needless to say, is the key to satisfying any fan base, whether it's Green Bay Packers Cheeseheads or wine-drinking San Francisco 49ers faithful, the Cleveland Browns Dawg Pound or the Oakland Raiders Black Hole denizens. They all react differently and negatively to defeat, so, as Al Davis, owner of the Raiders, said long ago, "Just win, baby."

"Jets fans? They are loyal—this is their team," Joe Benigno says. "I can't speak for everybody, but I think most fans feel the way I do. They feel we've waited long enough. This regime [the general manager Terry Bradway–coach Herman Edwards tandem] has done a nice job, I don't say they haven't, but at some point it's got to be about winning a championship. Anything short of the Super Bowl is not going to be good enough this year."

That's a high bar Joey B has set. But ask most Jets players and coaches, and they'd tell you they wouldn't want it any other way.

The New York Sack Exchange

Fans who have been following the Jets closely for as much as the past two decades must sometimes feel, in talking with Gang Green elders, as if the franchise has had only two epochs: the Namath era and the dark, soulless, Super Bowl–less age since. But there was another period in franchise history that, for a relative moment, almost matched Joe Namath's brilliance. That moment in the sun belonged to the "New York Sack Exchange."

Marty Lyons, one of the tackles on that dynamic Jets defensive line of the early eighties, remembered when the Sack Exchange, on which he was teamed with ends Joe Klecko and Mark Gastineau and tackle Abdul Salaam, began making group appearances around the New York area in 1981. "The first time we signed autographs as a unit, we did it at Macy's in Queens — I don't know how many hundreds of people showed up," Lyons said. "The next time, we did it at a sporting goods store in Port Jefferson. Joe and I pulled up together into the shopping center and there were *thousands* of people. I said, 'I can't believe all these people showed up for us.' And Joe said, 'Nah, they're here for a movie.' The lines circled all the way around the shopping center.

"It always feels good when you feel appreciated, and that was reflected in the way we played. We didn't want to disappoint ourselves or our teammates. Everybody has that in the back of his mind. And then the fans latched onto us as they did to Joe Namath, and we didn't want to disappoint them."

The only disappointment is that the Sack Exchange frenzy didn't last long enough — these fab four were brought together in 1979 but, due to injuries and trades, had only a two-year run together before the group devolved into Mark Gastineau's one-man show from 1983 to 1985. But the spirit of that group has lived on. Klecko and Gastineau were the star attractions, and whom you preferred said a lot about your personality. Did you like your football brawny, brawling, and blue collar? The short-haired Klecko was the call. Sexy, swift, and celebratory? The shaggy-maned Gastineau was your guy. Lyons and Salaam were the strong, silent types who plugged the gaps when opponents tried to run and freed up the sack masters when they tried to pass.

There were some tense times in the Sack Exchange's later days, mostly involving the flighty Gastineau, but when they were at their peak, they were a veritable Four Musketeers, one for all and all for one. That attitude continues to infuse the foursome even today. When the current Jets administration decided that on December 26, 2004, it would retire his uniform number 73—the first defensive player to receive that honor in franchise history—Klecko naturally was delighted. But he insisted his three line-mates accompany him to the 50 yard line for the ceremony at halftime of the game against the New England Patriots.

"When I got the call and they told me, it was overwhelming. I was shocked and surprised, but really, just so proud," he said. "I was proud to be recognized, but more proud of the fact that I would represent all the great teammates I had through the years and those teams that I played on. The more I thought about it, the more it really started to sink in. I played with a lot of great football players."

Like all great units with catchy nicknames, the Sack Exchange came together with a little planning, a little luck, and at first, no nickname. Walt Michaels was Lou Holtz's defensive coordinator in 1976, then after Holtz bolted, Michaels took the head-coaching reins and he and director of player personnel Mike Hickey brought the pieces together one by one.

Salaam was the first to arrive, in the seventh round in 1976 (when drafts lasted seventeen rounds) from Kent State. Actually he first came aboard as Larry Faulk but changed his name to Abdul Salaam, which means "soldier of peace," the next season.

I covered the team for one season in 1980, and even with the edgy natures of Klecko and linebacker Greg Buttle, possibly the scariest guy in the locker room was Salaam, who usually could be seen sitting and glowering in front of his locker, keeping many reporters at arm's length. Then Salaam had a standout game and the next day it was time to surround him for a mass interview. He turned out to be a friendly, engaging guy.

"Abdul," one reporter said, "we didn't think you liked us." "Hey, I didn't think *you* guys liked *me*," he replied.

Klecko came next, as a sixth-rounder in 1977 out of Temple, and that low status no doubt helped lay the foundation for the Exchange's trademark attitude. "I tell you, my first day after being drafted, I was very upset," he recalled. "I really thought I was a little better than a sixth-rounder, and I came in with a chip on my shoulder. There was nobody on two legs I wouldn't fight."

In 1979 Lyons was taken in the first round, fourteenth overall, out of Alabama, and Gastineau followed in the second round, forty-first overall, from tiny East Central in Ada, Oklahoma. Actually, Gastineau had bounced around, from Eastern Arizona Junior College to Arizona State, before landing at East Central. He first caught Hickey's eye when he was named the North's outstanding defensive lineman in the 1978 Senior Bowl. (Lyons earned the same honor for the South in the same college all-star game.)

"That's what you call drafting. We were geniuses. That's the way to do it," Michaels rightly crowed twenty-six years later from his Pennsylvania farm in March of 2005. "Marty was a steady player, there when you needed him. He fit in perfectly with Joe on the right side. And Mark was a great pass rusher, flamboyant—Abdul fit in perfect with him on the left side. Marty and Abdul snuck around, cleaned things up."

And behind the foursome, Michaels reminisced, Buttle was a "wild man" because he wanted to play some classic run defense. But because Gastineau would roar into the backfield, in the words of Jets offensive tackle Marvin Powell, "like it was the Indy 500," opponents would run inside Gastineau and suddenly Buttle was facing a wall of unblocked tackles and backs running their own race to find someone in green to run down. Michaels counseled Buttle thus: "Greg, you got to understand something. When they get an idea, you'd better let 'em go. Don't be asking them to play the run much."

While Gastineau was tearing loose on the left side of the defense, Lyons and Klecko had their own line of communications opened up on the right. "We didn't have any conversations," Lyons said. "We'd break the huddle, and if he saw the tackle split a little wider than usual, he'd just give me that Joe Klecko look. I knew what it was all about."

And in those days, Klecko was nearly as fast as Gastineau. "Joe beat a couple of fullbacks running, and Mark ran a legitimate 4.68 [seconds in the 40-yard dash]," Michaels said. "I didn't want them to run against each other much—they were such competitors. All you have to do is have them compete in a 40 and pull a muscle. I never let them run too many 40s. All they had to do was defeat the block and go to the play."

It wasn't the only time Michaels had to rein in his fantastic foursome. "Boy, they had excitement," he said. "The only guy who didn't show excitement—but you knew he was excited, too—was Abdul. Pregame, we'd come in after warming up, twelve to fifteen minutes before we'd have to go back out for introductions, and sometimes you didn't want to be near the door when they were ready. Between Marty and Joe, they could get excitable. But you don't want them using up energy. I'd say, 'Let's make it meaningful.'"

They quickly learned how to do that.

"If you were in third and long against us, those offensive linemen were shaking in their boots," Klecko said. "I forget which of the coaches said it while we were playing here: 'Who cares about blitzing when you have those four up there?' And that is what made it fun to play. We got after people. We got after people big time. And all four of us really complemented each other for what we did."

The group got cranking in 1980 when Gastineau led the team with 11.5 sacks and Klecko was right behind at 10.5. It was all a prelude for '81. The defense put together a decent eight sacks in the Jets' first three games, but they lost all three, giving up thirty-plus points each time. Then came Houston and the Oilers' two thirty-something quarterbacks, Ken Stabler and John Reaves, and the light changed to green. Gastineau had four sacks that day, the "D" totaled eight (and added six takeaways and a safety), and the Jets got off their schneid with a 33–17 victory.

Two games later, they racked up nine sacks—Klecko got a career-high 3.5 sacks plus the game ball—against the Patriots. Three games later came nine sacks of the Giants' Phil Simms. Two games after that, eight more at New England.

As the numbers mounted and the team got back on track toward a playoff berth, so did the hype surrounding the line. Like Minnesota's Purple People Eaters and Pittsburgh's Steel Curtain before them, this group was screaming out for an identity. Lyons remembered that assistant trainer Pepper Burruss put a chart up on the wall mapping the quartet's sack progress that season, and it sure did look like the chart of some corporation's stock price. At the same time, director of public relations Frank Ramos saw a fan in the stands holding up a bedsheet that read "New York Sack Exchange" and began incorporating the name in the weekly press releases.

Perhaps the fan with the sheet was Ed Lefkowitz, whom Michaels remembered was "a crazy Jets season-ticket holder" who also happened to be a stockbroker. "Ed got the idea and gave them the name," Michaels said. "They invited the four guys down there to the Stock Exchange, and they actually stopped trading for six minutes. People were calling from all over the world saying, 'What stopped the Stock Exchange?' It was the Sack Exchange." "That day," Lyons said, "was really overwhelming."

So was their last great game together, the 1981 regular-season finale against the Packers and Lynn Dickey, their statuelike quarterback. "The important part of that game was that if we won, we went into the playoffs, but if we lost, the Giants went into the playoffs," Lyons said. "I don't know how many times we sacked Dickey before halftime. He had no mobility—you knew he was going to be right back there between the guards. Then after the game, the fans rushing the field, tearing down the goal posts, to be a part of that . . . unfortunately, we never made it to the Super Bowl, so memories like that made us realize how fortunate we were."

The Jets did make the playoffs at 10–5–1. Klecko finished with 20.5 sacks and Gastineau with 20, and the Jets wound up with 66 sacks, at the time the second-most in NFL history to the 67 of the 1967 Raiders. But they lost at Shea to the Bills in their first postseason game since the 1969 season, 31–27.

After the Closing Bell

Here are the sack totals of the four members of the New York Sack Exchange, year by year as Jets:

	Gastineau	Klecko	Lyons	Salaam
UNOFFICIAL*				
1976	–	–	–	0
1977	–	8	–	4
1978	–	8	–	2
1979	2	7	3	2.5
1980	11.5	10.5	4.5	1
1981	20	20.5	6	7
OFFICIAL*				
1982	6	2	1.5	2.5
1983	19	6.5	4	0
1984	22	3	2	–
1985	13.5	7.5	6.5	–
1986	2	4	3	–
1987	4.5	1	3.5	–
1988	7	–	7.5	–
1989	–	–	1	–
OFFICIAL TOTALS	74	24	29	2.5
TOTALS	107.5	78	42.5	19

* The NFL first began tracking sacks officially in 1982.

The next season, Klecko ruptured his patella tendon early, and Lyons severely pulled his hamstring late. They both sucked it up, as they and everyone else knew they would, to return for the play-off run that took the Jets all the way to Miami and the "Mud Bowl," where they lost to the Dolphins, 14–0, in the AFC title game.

Within days, Michaels was fired and Joe Walton elevated to head coach. The next off-season, Salaam and backup defensive end Kenny Neil were traded, and the Sack Exchange electricity was gone. At least Gastineau danced his way to 22 sacks in 1984, the NFL record until Michael Strahan of the Giants, with help from Green Bay quarterback Brett Favre on the last weekend of the season, reset the bar at 22.5 in 2001. (Perhaps Favre's complicity in the sack was psychic payback for the shabby treatment of fellow Packers quarterback Dickey twenty years earlier!)

An interesting sidelight to this reveling in the joy of sacks is the NFL's ambivalence toward the statistic. Although the league kept team defensive sack stats back into the sixties, individual sacks have been recognized only since 1982, due, says the Elias Sports Bureau, to problems in combing through old play-by-plays and NFL Films footage and sorting out the wild inconsistencies in awarding sacks before that season.

This is a perhaps uncorrectable injustice most often railed against by former Los Angeles Rams end Deacon Jones. Jones has said he had 26 sacks in 1967, and the accounting of dedicated sack researcher John Turney gave him 173.5 for his fourteen-year career. Yet because that career ended in 1974, Jones officially has no sacks. As for the Jets, that means Klecko's 20.5-sack 1981 season doesn't officially exist, and Gastineau is credited with 107.5 career sacks even though he had 33.5 more that just don't count.

Of course the numbers wouldn't take on such importance if only there was some official acknowledgment of the Sack Exchange, say, by the Pro Football Hall of Fame. Gastineau's sack totals, both official and unofficial, are the best of the group, but because he ignored the run and then had many postcareer legal problems, he won't be going to Canton unless he drives himself there and purchases a ticket.

But Klecko has the credentials, the body of work. He will forever retain the distinction of being the first player selected to the Pro Bowl at three different positions (end, tackle, and nose tackle). It has become a cause célèbre for many to see number 73 not just retired on the green wall surrounding Giants Stadium on game days but also to have it enshrined in the Hall, starting with his fellow Sack Exchange members. "All three of us really believe Joe should be in the Hall of Fame," said Lyons, now the team's

Joe Klecko (left) wanted his linemates with him when his jersey was retired.
Bill Kostroun/AP

radio analyst. The Jets' organization feels the same way, having retired Klecko's number with an eye toward jump-starting his Hall of Fame candidacy.

Others outside the club are joining the chorus. Vic Carucci of Sirius NFL Radio and NFL.com, says, "Joe Klecko belongs in the Hall of Fame because he was a dominant defensive lineman, and the top qualification for Hall of Fame status should be a player's dominance at a given position."

"I have been in Joe's corner ever since he became eligible for enshrinement," Paul Zimmerman of *Sports Illustrated* says. "I believe it is a major oversight that this great player is not in the Hall of Fame."

Zimmerman's voice is one of the most important on this subject—he is the Jets' presenter, their mouthpiece, in front of the Hall's thirty-nine-member selection committee every January. But if only it were up to "Dr. Z." Vinny DiTrani of *The Record* of Hackensack, New Jersey, the Giants' presenter and a selection-commitiee member of the Hall of Fame since 1999, explains the arcane process that has stymied Klecko since he became eligible for enshrinement five years after his retirement in 1988, having played his last season with Indianapolis.

"The process starts out each year with hundreds of names, just about every player who's eligible," DiTrani explains. "The field gets cut to twenty-five, then to fifteen. That gets him 'in the room' the day of the voting [traditionally the day before each year's Super Bowl]. That day there are presentations, then we cut to ten and to six, and then it's a yes-no vote as to who gets in.

"Joe's a guy I would consider. I usually vote for him as one of my fifteen, but he just hasn't gotten there. Why, I don't know. I think part of his problem is that he's connected to Gastineau, kind of like Harry Carson's problem because he and Lawrence Taylor were linebackers together with the Giants."

It could also be an anti–New York bias, something that is believed to have reared its head in the selection meeting in the past. Maybe Klecko having only twenty-four "official" sacks hurts him, and up until 2004 maybe the fact that his number hadn't been retired by his team.

While DiTrani said he'd have to be convinced that Klecko deserves his yea vote should he ever become a finalist, he rates Klecko as just as valid a candidate as, say, Elvin Bethea, the defensive end of the Oilers who retired in 1983, couldn't get "in the room" until 2003, then was immediately voted into the Hall.

It doesn't seem that Klecko has hurt his candidacy by threatening any of the voters. As he said before his jersey retirement, "There's not many people I won't fight, but there's a soft side to you, too." He seems to be in a mellow mood these days, enjoying being Joe Klecko and taking the recognition when and where it comes.

"The Hall of Fame? That would be the pièce de résistance, as they say. If I was ever recognized in that realm, that would mean everything for a guy," Klecko said. "I'm a realist, I live in a realistic world. Accolades have never been a big deal for me. But for my family and my friends around me, being able to hang that Hall of Fame next to my name, that would be absolutely awesome."

And it would be a fitting tribute for a few awesome seasons that made Jets fans everywhere forget about Namath, just for a while.

A Thanksgiving of Pain

Injuries? This is the NFL. Every team has its injury sob stories, its painful tales of woe. As former Bills defensive end Bruce Smith, tormentor of Jets quarterbacks twice a year for fifteen years, said with only slight hyperbole, "I'm in a car crash every play."

So it's really of only passing significance to talk about Vinny Testaverde's ruptured right Achilles tendon in the 1999 opener against New England, crippling not only the venerable quarter-back but the Jets' entire season. Yes, the Jets were rudderless on offense until Bill Parcells installed Ray Lucas under a tight leash at quarterback at midseason. Yes, some opponents were saying they were glad the Jets at 8–8 had missed the playoffs. But every team has a season disfigured by the loss of one or more key per-formers. And no one can take away Testaverde's glorious 1998 season.

As for Joe Namath's injuries, they could make for a stirring chapter in a sports medicine textbook: the five knee surgeries, the broken wrist in 1970, the shoulder separation in '73. Just read *New York Times* columnist Dave Anderson's recounting in *Countdown to Super Bowl* of the syringes Namath needed to remove fluid and inject painkiller just so he could play the game on any given Sunday in the late sixties, before his knees got "really bad." But at least Broadway Joe won the big one. At least Namath left a legacy.

Most teams even have one of those tragedies such as the Vikings experienced in 2001 when big offensive tackle Korey Stringer died of heat stroke early in training camp. A lot was rightly made of Stringer's death at the time. And much more could have easily been made of the one player death in the his-tory of the Jets franchise. Except that Howard Glenn, a backup guard for the Titans, died in 1960, when reporting on pro foot-ball was a vastly different enterprise than it is today. Bill Ryczek in *Crash of the Titans* provides the mind-boggling details sur-rounding this death:

Glenn apparently broke his neck October 2 at Dallas when he suffered a seemingly minor injury, yet needed some time to

Vinny Testaverde tore
his Achilles tendon on
opening day in 1999.
John Greilick/AP

come around. The next game, back in the state of Texas, after a week of reportedly minimal treatment, Glenn was sent in to play against Houston. He was double-teamed on one play and had to be helped to the sideline, where he appeared fatigued and sullen. (Some players believed Glenn had been taking Benzedrine—"Bennies"—to enhance his performance.) He should have been examined by a team physician, but the Titans didn't travel with a doctor.

Glenn collapsed in the locker room and was taken to a Houston hospital. Coach Sammy Baugh told his players as their charter plane sat on the tarmac in Houston that Glenn had died. Television newscasts reported only that a Titans player had died, leaving family members and friends to guess if their loved one was okay until the charter landed and players ran to pay phones to call home.

That's enough fodder to keep cable television, Internet sites, and a Congressional panel humming for a week or more, had Glenn died forty-five years later.

But the Jets do have another catastrophic injury story to tell. The catastrophe was not that anybody died, but that two highly productive starters had their NFL careers snuffed out almost simultaneously. "It was," said one team insider who saw it all unfold, "an unbelievable couple of days."

The players were wide receiver Al Toon and defensive end Dennis Byrd. And in Toon's case at least, it wasn't any one injury that did him in. It was many concussions.

When Toon came to town, the future was bright for him and for the Gang Green offense. By virtue of their 7–9 record the year before, the Jets had the tenth pick overall in the 1985 draft. And by virtue of a passing attack that was led by a tight end (Mickey Shuler's 68 catches) and a wideout corps headed by the often-injured Wesley Walker and the almost-done Johnny "Lam" Jones, they were in the market for a wide receiver.

And the market was brimming with first-round wideout talent. There was the well-known 6', 185-pounder from the University of Miami, Eddie Brown, and a little-known 6'2", 200-pounder from tiny Mississippi Valley State by the name of Jerry Rice. And there was Toon. He had the best size of the threesome at 6' 4", 200 pounds, and he also had the best athletic résumé: record-setting pass-catcher for Wisconsin, MVP in the postseason all-star games after his senior season, and All-American track standout and a qualifier in the triple jump at the U.S. Olympic trials.

The Jets were the first of three teams in the draft in love with the wideouts. They took Toon at number ten, followed by the Bengals, who went with Brown at number thirteen, and the 49ers, who gobbled up Rice at number sixteen.

And the Jets were singing a happy tune in the months before the start of the 1985 season. "Al gives us the big, strong, durable wide receiver that everybody looks for," Coach Joe Walton said. "He should be an excellent third-down, possession-type receiver." "The thing that impressed us the most," added Mike Hickey, director of player personnel, "was that Al just loves to play football."

In retrospect, of course, the Jets should have been all over Rice, considered today the best wide receiver in the history of the game, who played more than a decade longer than his other two first-round draftmates. And Hickey had been known to take a flyer on a small-school player, although not generally in the first round.

Al Toon by the Numbers

Year		No	Yds	Avg	TD
1985	N.Y. Jets	46	662	14.4	3
1986	N.Y. Jets	85	1,176	13.8	8
1987	N.Y. Jets	68	976	14.4	5
1988	N.Y. Jets	93	1,067	11.5	5
1989	N.Y. Jets	63	693	11.0	2
1990	N.Y. Jets	57	757	13.3	6
1991	N.Y. Jets	74	963	13.0	0
1992	N.Y. Jets	31	311	10.0	2
TOTALS		517	6,605	12.8	31

But the Jets were happy with Toon, an intelligent family man who loved skiing and golf, basketball and jazz. And Toon began producing out of the gate with a franchise record for a rookie: 46 receptions. With at least one catch in the final nine games that season, he began a streak that ultimately reached 101 consecutive games with a catch.

From 1986 to 1988 he was almost unstoppable. In that time he *averaged* a season of 82 receptions for 1,073 yards and 6 touchdowns. He had an NFL-leading 93 receptions in 1988, still a franchise record. A simple 5-yard end-zone corner grab off a third-down audible from quarterback Ken O'Brien in the final regular-season game gave the Jets an 8–7–1 record and, equally important, defeated the Giants 27–21 and knocked them out of the playoffs. All three seasons he was voted the team's MVP by his teammates and played in the Pro Bowl.

But in expertly performing that third-down role Walton foresaw, beginning in earnest in 1988, Toon began to wear down. In 1989 a shoulder sprain knocked him out of the season opener. Two sprained ankles—in the same game!—cost him four midseason games. He also had a thigh contusion. Most significantly, he suffered his first NFL concussion, or at least the first one we know about.

Although Toon kept making the catches and moving the chains, he now was beginning to rack up more troubling numbers. He sat out the 1991 opener with a concussion, and his world was rocked to its core after his only catch at Denver—his last catch, as it turned out—on November 8, 1992.

One report said Toon believed it was his ninth concussion; another said he thought it was his thirteenth. Either number is shocking on its face, although NFL players at all positions will tell you that those numbers mean little because concussions happen all the time. But some players suffer from the effects of violent impacts on their brains more than others. In the weeks after the Broncos game, Toon's symptoms weren't going away, and the phrase "postconcussion syndrome" was beginning to get wide circulation around the NFL. Finally, on Friday, November 27, Toon announced his retirement from football.

That was the same day players around the NFL were talking about another severe trauma suffered by another one of their own. The year before, Detroit guard Mike Utley was upended, landed on his head and neck, and was paralyzed. During halftime ceremonies at the Lions' traditional Thanksgiving Day game in 1992, Utley was being honored. One of the awestruck players was Jets defensive lineman Dennis Byrd, who that week had told a reporter, "God, can you imagine what that must be like, spending the rest of your life in a wheelchair?"

Two days later, two days after Toon called it a career, Byrd suffered a Bruce Smith–style head-on crash with teammate Scott Mersereau while playing Kansas City at Giants Stadium.

Byrd entered the NFL five years earlier, with almost the same status as Toon. Byrd was a second-round pick in the 1989 draft, the forty-second player taken overall, a religious, community-minded, outdoors-loving lineman from Tulsa, and one of the few second-round picks the team got right during its fifteen-year stretch of "Terrible Twos." Defensive line coach Wallace Chambers, a former first-round defensive tackle himself, taken by the Bears in 1973 when he used to be known as Wally, had high praise for Byrd. "Dennis was the quickest end I worked out before the draft," Chambers said. "What he offers us is a total player, not a specialist. He's a throwback to the linemen who play every down. He's got the quickest hands I've seen in some time."

Byrd enjoyed a strong first season as a pass-rushing end—his 7 sacks were the most by a Jets rookie since Joe Klecko's 8 a dozen years earlier. With a frame listed at 6' 5" and 270 pounds, it was a little surprising that when defensive coordinator Pete Carroll joined the staff being formed by new head coach Bruce Coslet in 1990, Carroll moved Byrd to tackle.

But it was the "eagle" tackle position, the one from which Carroll had launched Keith Millard for 18 sacks with the Vikings the previous season, and Byrd immediately took flight. He started all thirty-two games in 1990 and 1991, notching 13 sacks in 1990—the most by any NFL interior lineman that year—and 7 more the next season. He had quickly become one of the NFL's top young sack hunters.

Yet Byrd clearly was struggling to maintain weight, having dipped to 254 pounds, linebacker size, before bulking up to a more muscular, yet leaner, 266. Carroll turned him into his left end in 1992, and although the idea was sound, for various reasons the production wasn't there.

The offense, with Browning Nagle struggling in his one season as the starting quarterback, was one of the worst in franchise history, and that always has an effect on the defense's performance. Through the first eleven games, the Jets struggled to a 3–8 record. Byrd missed three of the games with a shoulder injury and didn't have a single sack in the other eight.

But against the Chiefs and quarterback Dave Krieg, Byrd was making up for lost time. He already got his first sack of the season, and early in the third quarter, he was bearing down on Krieg's open side for sack number two. Unfortunately, Scott Mersereau, on a stunt from his left tackle spot, was doing the same thing from Krieg's blind side. When Krieg stepped up in the pocket, fumbling the ball, Byrd's helmet was driven into Mersereau's chest. Mersereau was on the Giants Stadium turf for two minutes. Byrd lay there much longer.

Much has been written since about the scene, most vividly in Byrd's autobiography, *Rise and Walk*. He knew his neck was broken. Trainer Pepper Burruss and team physicians Elliot Pellman, Stephen Nicholas, and Elliott Hershman stabilized him, from field to cart to ambulance to hospital, and saved his life. He

Dennis Byrd visits the Jets sidelines, years after his career ended in 1992.
Eric Miller/AP

was unable to move all week at New York's Lenox Hill Hospital—until he flexed his big toe, information that Dr. Nicholas passed on to Byrd's teammates on their charter flight to Buffalo. The seventeen-point-underdog Jets went on to score an amazing 24–17 road upset of the Super Bowl–bound Bills. Nicholas returned to Byrd's hospital room that night from the return flight and presented Byrd with the game ball.

Together, the Toon and Byrd situations represent the most traumatic time in the Jets' history. Yet, as Frank Ramos, then the team's director of public relations, recalled, the importance of losing two starters in their prime in a three-day span didn't sink in right away. "I don't think anybody thought of it as the Jets were reeling from that," said Ramos, who always did his best work during his team's times of crisis. "The injuries were actually very different in a way. In Al's case, you really thought he was going to get better eventually. It took longer than anybody thought, but to this day people don't know that much about concussions and how dangerous they are. Players used to say, 'Oh, that guy's just seeing stars,' and people would use poor terminology to describe concussions, when you think about it now.

"Byrd's injury was life-threatening at the time. We were wondering right then if he was ever going to be able to move again."

While Byrd slowly began his rehabilitation back home in Oklahoma, Toon retired to his Wisconsin farm, where he continued to show irritability, fatigue, and sensitivity to light and couldn't even watch his children ride a merry-go-round without getting dizzy.

But eventually both players got back on their feet. Within a year Byrd was standing and walking haltingly. And he began his postfootball career, starting up the Dennis Byrd Foundation, one of whose main goals was building a 470-acre camp for physically challenged kids in central Oklahoma.

"I try to help out wherever I can," Byrd said more than five years later, when he returned to the Jets' complex in July 1998. The visit, scheduled weeks earlier, was to watch training camp practice and chat with Jets coach Bill Parcells. But as luck would have it, he was in the area to help out when a Chinese gymnast, seventeen-year-old Sang Lan, was paralyzed after breaking her neck while practicing for her performance in the Goodwill Games, being held literally across the street at Nassau Coliseum.

Despite being minutes away from the Nassau County Medical Center in East Meadow, New York, Byrd said he has always felt it "somewhat presumptuous" to drop in unannounced on a patient he didn't know. But he received an invitation from the Chinese Gymnastic Association and left a news conference in the Jets' facility to meet with Sang.

It was not unlike visits Byrd had with actor Christopher Reeve; former Detroit Lions linebacker Reggie Brown, paralyzed in the 1997 regular-season finale against the Jets, and Mike Utley. He sends out "a couple of hundred" letters a year to paralysis victims and draws inspiration from visits to his Owasso, Oklahoma, home from some of his correspondents.

Despite having lost forty pounds from his playing weight, Byrd that day still cut an impressive figure on the sideline during practice and as he hugged former teammates and opponents such as linebackers Mo Lewis and Pepper Johnson and offensive tackle Siupeli Malamala. He was walking then, but still had work

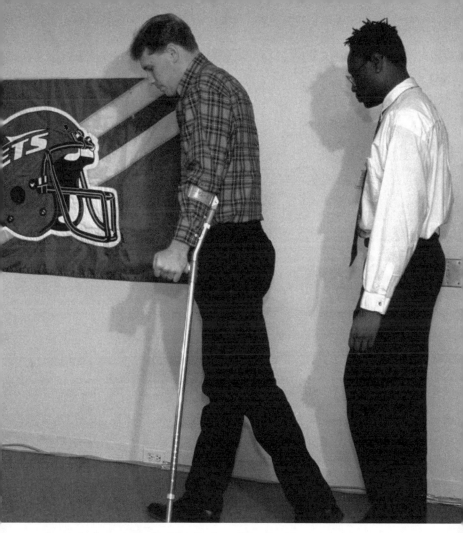

Dennis Byrd rose and walked despite the collision that almost killed him.
Marty Lederhandler/AP

ahead of him. His stride was slow, with a stiff right step, then a trembling left step, on legs more slender than one would expect from a once-rising pass-rush star. "I have pain—it's called central nerve pain," he said. "It's in my feet and hands and hips. It's like a sunburn. I feel that most of the time. I suffer from fatigue and muscular weakness. I'm still not able to jog."

Somehow, though, Byrd's outlook was far from being fatigued. His religious convictions—expressed the day of his injury when he told the team's doctors and his wife Angela, "Thank you, Lord Jesus, for putting me in this position because you know I'm strong enough to stand it"—were as strong as ever. "Obviously, it was a day that changed my life," he said. "There are times you cringe and thoughts go through your mind, but not in a sad way. It's hard to convince people that when something happens like this, you won't look back and be bitter. I'm just thankful for what I have. I'm very blessed."

"To remember what he went through and the feeling and emotions that we shared, that's a pretty powerful feeling," said Malamala, a rookie the year Byrd was hurt. "It's great to see him out here with that smile on his face."

Toon is smiling again, too. He publicly emerged from the depths of his postconcussion syndrome in September 2004, when he participated in his first Wisconsin Ironman triathlon. That competition consists of a 2.4-mile swim, 112 miles of bicycling, and a 26.2-mile marathon run. Toon, the former world-class athlete, finished 1,343rd in a field of 2,188. Suffice it to say that he didn't get the gold, silver, or bronze that day, but medals were the furthest thing from his mind.

"Being a professional football player was an awesome feat, and so was qualifying for the Olympic trials. But doing something I didn't feel I was really built to do was very special," Toon said. In completing the last leg of the Ironman, the marathon, he said he had "no problems" running the longest distance of his life. "At about 20 miles, I said, 'You know what? I'm going to finish. I feel great.'"

News like that can only make followers of one of the most difficult times in Jets history feel great as well.

For Chrebet, the Fight Is Not Over

Today Wayne Chrebet is in daddy mode, keeping tabs on sons Lukas and Cade in his spacious home not far from the Jersey shore while his wife, Amy, is out. He talks with a friend about the latest chapter in his career, the one in which reports of his demise, similar to that of Mark Twain a little over one hundred years before, were greatly exaggerated.

"It's just a shame. Some people write that my career is over, the Jets are going to let me go, then it catches on, people start talking about it on the radio," said Chrebet, the team's Everyman wide receiver. "I never really said anything about it. I needed to take time, obviously, to see how I felt, but also to see where I stood with the team, with the doctors, with my family. That's all I said and it kind of went from there—'sources close to the situation.' They got some janitor at the complex saying I wasn't coming back."

The "it" Chrebet refers to is the NFL's "c" word, *concussion*. He lost the second half of the 2003 season to postconcussion syndrome, and he had to sit out the San Diego playoff game in January of 2005 because he took a blow to the head in the regular-season finale at St. Louis. Chrebet is not at former wide receiver Al Toon's mile marker on the concussion highway yet (Toon suffered at least nine concussions before his early retirement), but he knows he's somewhere on that road, and it brings a chill to his football player's heart.

"I've always felt I could fight through anything," he said. "This is the first time in my life I'm fighting something I don't understand, something I can't see. It would be tough to swallow if that ends up being the reason I have to walk away from the game sooner than I would want to. If it weren't for that, in the right place I think I could play years more. I'm only thirty-one. I'm as fresh as can be for a guy going into his eleventh year."

Eleven seasons in the NFL. Not bad for this average-looking 5' 10", 185-pounder from the North Jersey suburbs and the college he calls "Nowhere University, by football standards"—actually Hofstra University, also the home of the Jets training complex. Chrebet's NFL career has had a number of chapters. And the first, in some ways, is the funniest and the most instructive about what he's all about.

Rich Kotite had just become head coach of the Jets, at the behest of owner Leon Hess, who remembered seeing him "bust a gut trying to get plays in from the coaches' box" when he was an assistant coach in the 1980s. Kotite's idea was to get his new team off and running with a two-tight-end offense, especially after taking Kyle Brady with the first pick of the 1995 draft to team with Johnny Mitchell. But he still needed wide receivers— lots of them.

Chrebet was one of those wideouts. The Jets knew about him from Hofstra, but he and Art Weiss, his agent then and now, still had to battle just to get a league-minimum $119,000 contract, including a $1,500 signing bonus. His next battle was getting past Harry Fisher at the team's first full-squad minicamp after the draft.

Who's Harry Fisher? A guard. Specifically, at that time he was the lone security guard who stood patrol at the entrance to the team complex. Harry was a large man and always dressed the security guard part with a trooper's hat, shades, and tan uniform. He had a voice like frozen gravel even in casual conversation, but when a potential law-breaker was afoot, he would bellow a blood-curdling "*Haaallllt!*" right out of *COPS*.

Chrebet heard that voice April 28, 1995, when he reported for his first day of work as a pro football player. "A lot of legends and stories about me have grown, but the Harry Fisher story hasn't gotten embellished," Chrebet recalled. "That day I had on shorts and a backpack, and I was wearing my hat low. Harry had chased a

Numbers Game

Wayne Chrebet wore uniform number 3 at Hofstra because he and two other close friends took the numbers 1, 2, and 3. With the Jets he initially settled on number 3 because, with so many wide receivers in camp, there were no numbers available in the eighties or in the teens. Here are the nine other receivers Chrebet was in competition with for a roster spot on the 1995 Jets and how they broke in:

Stevie Anderson, Cardinals eighth-round draft choice, 1993

Ryan Yarborough, Jets second-round draft choice, 1994

Orlando Parker, Jets fourth-round draft choice 1994

Tyrone Davis, Jets fourth-round draft choice, 1995

Curtis Ceaser, Jets seventh-round draft choice, 1995

Alan Allen, training camp (with Jets), 1994

Tom Garlick, training camp (with Eagles), 1994

Chad Askew, Jets undrafted free agent, 1995

Brian Sallee, Jets undrafted free agent, 1995

Of the nine only Anderson, Yarborough, Parker, Davis, and Ceaser played in the NFL. Including Davis's eight seasons, 69 games, and 73 catches, 13 for touchdowns, as a tight end for the Jets and the Packers, the nine combined to play in 149 regular-season games and make 134 catches, 17 for touchdowns. Chrebet in his career has played in 144 games with 565 catches, 41 for touchdowns.

couple of kids looking for autographs in front of me, and he just didn't get it that I was there for the minicamp."

Fisher, who retired after the 1997 season, dropped in on the 1999 minicamp and reminisced about apprehending this intruder. "I said, 'Where do you think you're going?' He said he was going into the complex and I said, 'Like hell you are,'" Fisher said. "He said, 'I'm Wayne Chrebet,' so I said, 'Yeah, and I'm Jesus Christ Superstar.' Then I called in and was told to let him in. I apologized. I felt like a jerk. We've joked about it since then. He said, 'Being from Hofstra, I thought you would've ticketed my car.' I said, 'If I knew it was your car, I would've had it towed away.'"

Chrebet said in subsequent visits, "When I walked back to the dorms with icepacks taped all over me, Harry would say, 'You got the ice? I'll get the gin.'"

Soon Chrebet could pop the Korbel. Even though it has been said he was tenth on the ten-man depth chart at wide receiver that summer, he really was tied for eighth with two other undrafted rookie free agents, but the veterans and draft choices ahead of him were a motley crew. Chrebet had a strong training camp and a modest final three preseason games with 9 receptions (for 91 yards) that still led all wide receivers. Not only did he make the roster, but he also made the opening-day starting lineup at Miami.

Some have argued that starting a Hofstra free agent at flanker that year was one of many misdeeds Kotite perpetrated against the Jets, their fans, and the NFL. Other sins included putting together one of the worst passing offenses in league history; starting inexperienced Everett McIver at left tackle in a pinch at Buffalo, which led to Bills defensive end Bruce Smith blasting

Wayne Chrebet has an urgency to get every last inch out of each catch.

Kathy Willens/AP

quarterback Boomer Esiason clear into Monday; and some days slipping out almost before practice was over to get in nine holes of golf.

Oh, yeah, and there were the 3–13 and 1–15 records the Jets compiled under his watch. The combined winning percentage of .125 is one of the nine worst marks in back-to-back seasons since the 1970 merger.

Kotite was roundly vilified, but two positives from his rule are undeniable: He paved the way for Hess to begin pulling strings to bring Bill Parcells aboard, and he gave Wayne Chrebet an opportunity. "Obviously, Richie has a place in my heart. He saw something in me that was there but that not many other people saw," Chrebet said. "For whatever reason I still don't know, he gave me a chance, and I didn't want to let him down."

There was another Kotite trait that Chrebet admired. "I couldn't believe the freedom Richie gave us," he said. "He treated us like men. It just didn't work out. The worst part about it was we had a good team, but we just could not catch a break, and that last year got worse and worse. And the thing about him was he stood up for us, never blamed us, and took it on himself every week. At the end he was basically tarred and feathered, and he never pointed a finger at us. That's a true man, right there. That's why I love him."

Kotite clearly felt the same. "Wayne," he said simply the September after he "stepped aside" as the coach of the Jets, "is the kid I never had."

During those first two years, Chrebet began working on his legend. His first pro catch, he said, was one of his five all-time toughest, a corner route out of the slot from Esiason—he latched onto the back end of the ball and held on for dear life as he went out of

Wayne Chrebet by the Numbers

Here are Wayne Chrebet's career receiving statistics with the Jets:

SEASON	Games	Recs	Yards	Avg	TD
1995	16	66	726	11.0	4
1996	16	84	909	10.8	3
1997	16	58	799	13.8	3
1998	16	75	1,083	14.4	8
1999	11	48	631	13.1	3
2000	16	69	937	13.6	8
2001	15	56	750	13.4	1
2002	15	51	691	13.5	9
2003	7	27	289	10.7	1
2004	16	31	397	12.8	1
TOTALS	144	565	7,212	12.7	41
PLAYOFFS					
1998	2	12	166	13.8	0
2001	1	4	52	13.0	2
2002	2	3	51	17.0	0
2004	1	0	0	—-	0
TOTALS	6	19	269	14.2	2

bounds for a 27-yard gain. His first pro touchdown came the next week against Indianapolis on a 5-yard Esiason needle-threader.

He had 8 catches for 98 yards against St. Louis in game 13 his rookie year, then topped that with career highs of 12 catches and 162 yards the next season at Jacksonville. Characteristically, the Jets lost both games.

The word from opponents in those days was to let Chrebet catch the ball—he wasn't going to hurt you and he had no one else to help him. That strategy may have worked for the Kotite Jets, but it also kept Chrebet's competitive juices flowing. "The impression may be that if I caught a 40-yard touchdown and someone else who was more impressive looking or a high draft pick caught the same pass, you would just view it differently," he said. 'But that was good. It just added fuel to my fire. If teams don't keep paying me much mind, it was quiet, but I'd just go about my business out there and the next thing you'd know, I was 5 for 100 and 4 more [converted] third downs. I just kind of snuck up on people. I like that. It's nice proving people wrong."

But not everyone was unpleasantly surprised. First, the number 80 jerseys began sprouting around the New York area. The fans loved Chrebet's sure hands, the way he gave up his body to make catches or block men one hundred pounds heavier, his relentless urgency at getting every last inch out of every catch, especially in converting third downs into first downs . . . They also loved the fact that he looked a lot like them.

"Right away I became the symbol of the underdog, which is fine by me," he said. "Then year after year, just seeing the amount of '80' jerseys in the stands and on the street, some of the fan mail I get, the people I meet . . . People come up to me and say the most outrageous stuff, but my dad [Wayne Sr.] said, 'Don't get offended by what people say to you. What they're saying is, "You make it look so easy, you make me think I can do it, too."' That made me understand what people think of me. It's all about giving people joy and hope, and I think I've done that."

Chrebet was about to be tested in the post-Kotite years by two new, larger-than-life Jets: Coach Bill Parcells and wide receiver Keyshawn Johnson.

Parcells was really a pushover—after all, he was coach of the Giants, Wayne and his family's team when he was a kid. They both grew up in lunch-pail sections of Bergen County, New Jersey. And they both wanted to win. All Chrebet had to do was survive Parcells's withering sarcasm, as captured in this one-liner early in their first season together in 1997: "Chrebet, your career is going downhill faster than a dump truck off a cliff with a cement parachute."

Then there was the Tuna injury rehab plan. Chrebet was standing on the sideline at a practice a week after he had suffered a bad high-ankle sprain in the third game of the season. Parcells was there to see how his wide receiver was doing, sort of: He launched a good kick to the inside of Chrebet's ankle. "If I could've put weight on the ankle then, I would've kicked him with my good foot," Chrebet said.

The impression has always been that Chrebet wanted to give a swift kick and more to Keyshawn Johnson, the first overall pick of the 1996 draft who arrived as a big-target wideout with big-time skills and a big mouth and attitude to match. The two clashed that first season and in succeeding years. Each took potshots at the other in their biographies and in the occasional newspaper or radio interview.

Chrebet may be guilty of revisionist history, but there is anecdotal evidence from the two combatants to suggest that they actually coexisted peacefully, as teammates and as next-door locker

Keyshawn Johnson (19) and Wayne Chrebet pushed each other for four seasons.
Alex Horvath/AP

mates. "Keyshawn was a really good player who I thought could be great if he let himself be," said Chrebet, adding about their relationship, "It was never as bad as people thought it was. If you go back and watch the games, we were killing for each other. That was the best part of it. We were so competitive in practice that we just got so much better without realizing it. On the field, it wasn't just, 'Can you catch this?' It was 'Can you block this? Can you do that?' He got a Super Bowl ring [with Tampa Bay]—he beat me to it. I'm jealous."

Johnson has publicly agreed with only half that assessment, that he made Chrebet a better player. And he uttered the classic bulletin-board line—"I'm a star, Wayne Chrebet's just a flashlight"—that backfired miserably when Chrebet made another one of his highlight catches, a last-minute, 18-yard snag of Curtis Martin's option pass for the game-winning touchdown in a 21–17 comeback win over Keyshawn's Bucs in 2000.

But Johnson, on a good day, recognized Chrebet's contributions. Here's what he said when I asked him about their relationship for *Sports Illustrated* in 1997:

"When I first came into the league, it was kind of weird to see Wayne playing in the positions where the Jets drafted a bunch of guys and signed guys as free agents," he said. "But after you look a year later and you see he's doing the same things he did a year ago, with a different staff, you've got to admire some of those things he does. We really don't have an off-the-field relationship. We speak, we talk, we joke, and that's it. The only people who tried to turn our relationship into something it wasn't was the media. They wanted to turn it into a worse competition than what it was."

Chrebet today sees even another silver lining to those sometimes stormy four seasons. "We weren't going to go out and have dinner, but the respect has always been there, maybe not initially, but once we had played together," he said. "Maybe one of the best things to happen to me from a national standpoint were the books. People would say, 'Who is this Chrebet guy?' After that, I got my name out there that much more."

For at least the 1998 season, the team of Chrebet and Johnson was one of the best wideout tandems in the NFL. Chrebet enjoyed the only 1,000-yard receiving season of his career and had his best per-catch average (14.4). Johnson has yet to match his 10 touchdown catches that season. And Chrebet got as close as he's ever come to the career-long goal that keeps him going, when the Jets played at Denver for the AFC championship and a Super Bowl berth.

But in the NFL, it rarely goes smoothly for any one player for very long. Chrebet's 1999 season was marred by close friend Vinny Testaverde tearing his Achilles tendon in the opener. In 2000 he was the Jets number-one receiver for the last time, but his good year couldn't get his team over a season-ending three-game losing streak that sent them home with no playoffs and sent coach Al Groh packing for the University of Virginia.

In the next chapter of the book of Wayne, he meets new coach Herman Edwards—good—and new coordinator Paul Hackett—bad.

Hackett always talked a good game regarding Chrebet, but usually it was along the lines of what the Jets needed to do that they hadn't been doing. Late in 2001, for instance, Hackett said about Chrebet's lessened opportunities, "For us to be at our best,

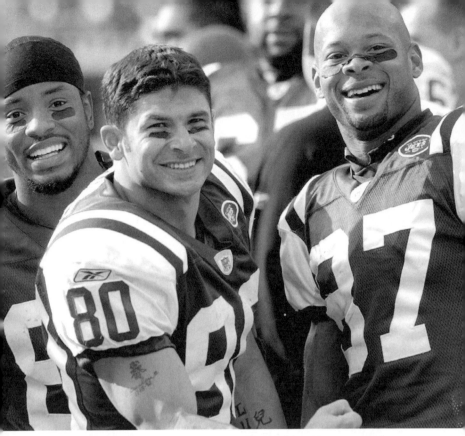

Wayne Chrebet with good friends Santana Moss (left) and Laveranues Coles.
Bill Kostroun/AP

from this point on, Wayne has to be in the middle of everything."

But from then until Hackett left the Jets after the 2004 season, Chrebet seemed to slowly be at the edge of everything. His production in 2003 and 2004 was the lowest of his first ten years. In 2004 he played in five games in which he didn't have a catch; he'd had three such games in his career before that.

"I try not to speak bad about people, but I just don't have anything really nice to say about the guy. When other people don't speak nicely of him, he's still a coach on my team. Maybe I won't defend the guy, but I don't want to hear it," Chrebet said. "But someone came up to me once and said, 'Hackett did to you what no DB could. He shut you down.' I didn't know this guy, but I said to myself, man, he's got a point."

All the frustration could go away for what may be Chrebet's final chapter. He has a new coordinator in Mike Heimerdinger, who's been known to stretch the field more and adjust on the fly better than the departed coordinator. And Coach Edwards appears to be on his side. "You're talking about a receiver who came in as a free agent and has caught 500 balls—he's had a wonderful career," Edwards said. "Players like Wayne are all looking for the same thing. They want to go out as champions. Now it's a matter of sitting down and figuring out the best way he can help us get it."

Another achievement in Chrebet's sights is Don Maynard's franchise record of 627 career receptions from 1960 to 1972. At 565 catches after 2004, there's a real question whether Chrebet can reach it. Perhaps he'll get help by being reunited with his old friend, Laveranues Coles, the wide receiver the Jets reluctantly allowed to depart for the Washington Redskins as a restricted free agent after the 2002 season, then traded for in March of 2005.

"Me and Laveranues, we were as tight as it got," Chrebet said. "He's a phenomenal player, he's still young, and he plays with a chip on his shoulder. That's why we get along—we both have that big old chip that we're not going to get rid of."

The Tuna Has Landed

Bill Parcells's first introduction as a member of the New York Jets in January 1997 was like something out of *Star Trek* or *Monty Python's Flying Circus*. Because New England owner Robert Kraft was contesting Parcells's departure from the Patriots without compensation, the NFL declared he couldn't become the Jets' coach or show up at their complex until its investigation was done.

But Leon Hess, the octogenarian oilman owner of the Jets, was eager to push the envelope and bring the Big Tuna aboard, so his lawyers came up with a brilliant strategy: Bill Belichick, who joined the Jets as defensive coordinator after his Patriots contract had expired, was designated acting head coach and Parcells was named an adviser to the team.

And so at the news conference in the second-floor auditorium of Weeb Ewbank Hall to announce the glorious transition from the Rich Kotite error (3–13 and 1–15 seasons) to the Parcells era, Belichick took the stage and sat down next to a table on which was a small pyramidal base with a metal bar sticking out— a conference call device that conveyed Parcells's voice to reporters via telephone hookup.

The tableau made for some light moments. In a week the NFL decided the Jets should pay the Patriots a stiff price: two first-round draft picks plus a second- and third-rounder to get Parcells out of his New England deal. Hess paid, Parcells appeared in person as the team's coach, and the good times continued to roll.

Then the next day the real Tuna, the all-business Tuna, came out. Parcells drove into the then-ungated parking lot at the team's Hofstra University complex at 6:00 A.M. for his first day of work as head coach and de facto general manager—and was greeted by Anthony Fucilli of MSG Network.

"What the [bleep] are you doing here?" Parcells snarled, clearly not in the mood for a chirpy stand-up interview.

"We just wanted to get some tape of you starting your first day," Fucilli replied.

"Well, enjoy it now," Parcells said over his shoulder, "because next week I'm putting up a [bleep]ing wall."

The new boss was true to his word. The parking lot was enclosed with a chain-link fence for the first time. Large parts of the first floor of the complex once open to reporters became restricted. Locker-room time was slashed, regular-season practices closed. Assistant coaches contractually were allowed to talk to the media only with permission of the head coach, which was rarely granted.

Bill was building another team, his way.

Vinny DiTrani, my compatriot as the beat writer covering the Giants for *The Record* and one of Parcells's closest confidants among the reporters who have covered him, has advanced through his seniority to become a member on the Pro Football Hall of Fame selection committee. In that capacity he presented Parcells for the committee's consideration in January of 2002.

"I described Bill as a mix between 'The Natural' and 'The Lone Ranger,'" DiTrani said. "He's a natural kind of coach. He knows what buttons to push, what things to do. It all comes naturally. But he also has that attitude that, 'Our job is done here, Tonto, let's move on.' I think he takes more pleasure in building a team than in keeping it. It doesn't mean every place he's gone has been downtrodden, and the outcome with the fourth one [the Dallas Cowboys] has yet to be determined, but he managed to get the first three to at least a championship game.

"He also wasn't having a good time with Bob Kraft in New England. He had to get out of there, and the Jets were ideal. I think at the time there was some talk that he could come back to the Giants, but that was nixed. If he couldn't come back to the Giants, the Jets were the next best place for him."

Carl Banks, Parcells's onetime Giants first-round draft choice who accompanied him to the Jets as director of player develop-

Bill Parcells and owner Leon Hess after the Jets landed the Big Tuna in 1997.
Kathy Willens/AP

ment, put it this way about his boss: "This is a man who thrives on misery. You know what I'm saying?"

Chad Cascadden knows exactly. "I don't think anybody out there can beat Bill up more than he beats himself up," said Cascadden, who occasionally starred as a role-playing linebacker for two seasons under Parcells and Belichick. "When he loses, he takes it personally. When he wins, he thinks we can do a better job. That makes you a great coach and motivator. I always appreciated his style because I thought it was fair."

Which is not to say Cascadden always agreed with how he was treated. For instance, Parcells was one of the first NFL coaches to lean hard on all his players to attend his off-season strength and conditioning program. Such programs typically run four days a week for ten weeks from March through May. Once upon a time, that was the players' time to chill with family, find off-season employment, and work out leisurely alone or with teammates before the heavy lifting began again in July.

Cascadden made the mistake, the first week of Parcells's first Jets off-season workout schedule, of having a family emergency. When he finally showed up, he recalled the conversation:

Cascadden: "I had something I had to take care of, Bill. But I'm here now. I'm not going anywhere."
Parcells: "Hey, don't tell me about the pain, show me the baby. I don't want to hear about your problems. Just get done whatever needs to get done."

"It was a bit cold," Cascadden recalled, "but I understood where he was coming from. I didn't take offense. This is a results-oriented guy."

Parcells had already bruised the feelings of holdover employees in Weeb Ewbank Hall who had grown up with the idea that the Jets and Giants were not friendly rivals. A few in the organization went back to the early sixties, when the then-AFL Titans found housing for many of their players in the Bronx Concourse Hotel, where many Giants players also lived; the Giants were ordered not to associate with the Titans. To this day the Jets hierarchy does contortions to avoid mentioning Giants Stadium in their press releases and in press-box announcements, even though that's been the name of their home venue since 1984. It's always "The Meadowlands."

But Tuna enlisted a number of ex-Giants to help him get the Jets back on their feet. Besides Banks and Belichick, he brought in coaches Romeo Crennel, Charlie Weis, Al Groh, Maurice Carthon, Pat Hodgson, and Mike Sweatman to join Ron Erhardt, former offensive coordinator with the Giants who was already on staff. Linebacker Pepper Johnson and guard William Roberts were reunited with tackle John "Jumbo" Elliott, who arrived a year earlier.

And Parcells advised everyone in no uncertain terms to quit bitching about playing in Giants Stadium. That's where they're playing their home games, no one's changing the name, so get over it.

Listening to Parcells during his first Jets training camp practices was worth the price of admission—except to the players who were the butt of his barbs: "You want to tell that player something? Tell him how to find the bus station, 'cause he's gonna need it!" . . . "You guys are a bunch of lazy bastards!" . . . "Let me tell you something. I don't have to get used to your [bleep]ing moods. You have to get used to my moods!"

"That's the way I coach—straightforward," Parcells explained in between camp workouts. "I tell the players what I think. Once in a while, if they get their feelings hurt, that's too bad. I get my feelings hurt when we lose. That's when I pout around a little bit."

Finally, August 31, 1997, arrived—Opening Day at Seattle. Losing was not in the game plan, and the Jets played as if shot out of cannons. They destroyed the Seahawks 41–3, posting the largest season-opening victory in franchise history. Everything went right, from Neil O'Donnell's five touchdown passes to the defense pitching a near shutout to rookie John Hall launching a franchise-record-tying 55-yard field goal with the first kick of his NFL career. "I'm happy with the way we played. We didn't make one really dumb play," Parcells grumped a day later. "It's one lousy game. Let's keep it in perspective."

The Jets lurched through the season as Parcells predicted. They sat at 8–4 after twelve games and in sole possession of first place in the AFC East that late in a season for the first time in more than a decade. Then they hit a slump with limp back-to-back losses to Buffalo and Indianapolis.

But just as everyone was burying their first season under Tuna, the Jets rocked playoff-bound Tampa Bay 31–0 in wind-tunnel conditions at the Meadowlands. Suddenly they were 9–6 and facing the most tantalizing of scenarios for a regular-season finale: The winner of their game at Detroit would make the play-offs; the loser would not.

Many Gang Green fans will never forgive Parcells for his decisions in the Pontiac Silverdome that day to take the ball out of O'Donnell's hands and give it to rookie Leon Johnson on a halfback-option pass and then to untested Ray Lucas at key junctures—both threw crushing interceptions. Barry Sanders broke free late to clear 2,000 rushing yards, and the Jets lost 13–10.

Regardless, the tone had been set. The team's eight-game turnaround was one of the best for a one-win team in NFL history. And 1998 beckoned. In fact Jumbo Elliott recalled his old/new coach offering, well, not a Namathian guarantee as much as a Parcellsian promise, in the dead of winter in a nearly empty weight room. "Bill promised me the playoffs then," Elliott remembered. "He was pretty much tired—9 and 7 doesn't cut it for him—and he said, 'I promise you we're going to be in the playoffs this year.'"

With the help of two handpicked Tuna imports—quarterback Vinny Testaverde, who took the reins from Glenn Foley permanently after a loss at St. Louis in the fifth game, and linebacker Bryan Cox—Parcells delivered on his promise. After a 2–3 start, the Jets won ten of their last eleven. A Sunday night, 21–16 win

Bill Parcells plucked Vinny Testaverde off the scrap heap for his 1998 title run.
Mike Derer/AP

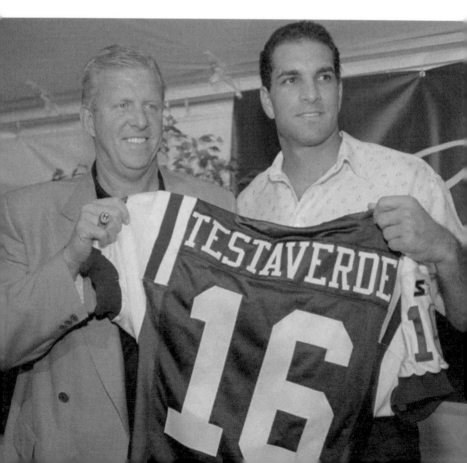

at Miami in game 14 clinched a playoff berth, then a 17–10 victory at Buffalo the next week earned the Jets their first division championship since before the 1970 NFL-AFL merger and brought tears to Parcells's eyes as he thanked his team in the cramped Rich Stadium locker room after the game.

Ray Mickens had a front-row seat for all of it, and he was a prime example of how Parcells molded that year's Jets into winners. Enjoying a strong season as the nickel back, Mickens was pressed into duty as the left cornerback starter when Aaron Glenn went down with a severe high ankle sprain against Seattle the week before the Miami win.

"Bill pulled me over after that game and put the onus on me," Mickens said. "He said, 'How well you play is going to decide whether we're going to win or lose these games.' I'm thinking to myself, 'Okay, if I play well, we'll win. If I don't, we'll lose. I don't want to be the reason we lose.' I put it on myself. I don't like to lose no matter what I do. From that day forward, we won every game all the way up to the championship game."

That included a season-ending rout of New England at home, then the Jets' first home playoff game since 1969, against Jacksonville. The Jets dominated the first half against the Jaguars, and on the strength of a second quarter in which they held the ball for more than fourteen minutes, they were about to take a 17–0 lead in at halftime—when, on the last play of the half, Jacksonville quarterback Mark Brunell found Jimmy Smith on a 52-yard touchdown pass.

Parcells and Belichick were livid, not so much at Otis Smith, the cornerback on the play, but at safety Jerome Henderson, who was supposed to be deeper than the deepest receiver but let

Smith get past him down the sideline. "That was crazy. We got tough on Jerome. He didn't want to leave the locker room after that," said one Jets player at the time. "Parcells doesn't like any type of mistakes, especially in a big game like that."

Not to worry. The Jags got no closer than seven down late as the Jets won 34–24, advancing to the conference title game against the Broncos in Denver for the right to represent the AFC in Super Bowl XXXIII. When they took a 3–0 lead into their Mile High Stadium locker room at intermission, Parcells warned his troops, "They're a great team. Stay on 'em."

And when Blake Spence made the biggest play of his short time as a Jet, blocking Tom Rouen's end-zone punt to set up Curtis Martin's 1-yard touchdown run 3:04 into the second half, the Jets had a 10–0 lead, and suddenly the dream became real. "I couldn't believe the season we were having, and then it was 10–0 and all I could think of was that I was going to be starting in the Super Bowl," Mickens said. "But then the second half was history with John Elway."

Elway and Terrell Davis took over from there, moving Denver from ten points down to ten ahead in a ten-minute span. When the Jets' 23–10 loss was in the books, Parcells publicly and privately fingered safety Victor Green for biting on a crossing pattern, freeing up Ed McCaffrey for a 47-yard reception from Elway that got the Broncos back in the game. But Parcells's hand-picked veterans also had their problems: Martin and Keith Byars each lost a fumble, David Meggett failed to cover a windblown kickoff, and Testaverde threw two late interceptions.

As bitter as the defeat was, the Jets had every reason to feel like they would be partying in 1999. Elway retired, and except for

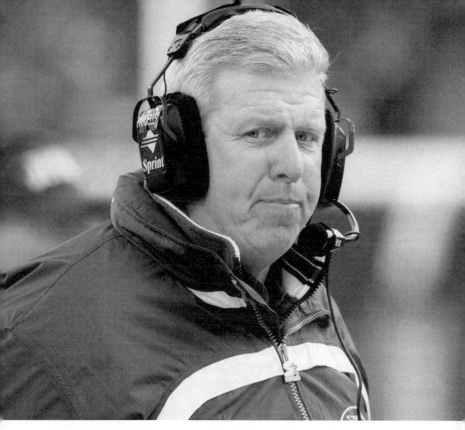

Not even a scowling Bill Parcells could end the Jets' championship drought.
Mark Lennihan/AP

wide receiver Wayne Chrebet, who broke his foot in the preseason, the Jets had all their key players back—until the season opener against New England. That's when they lost Testaverde for the year when, untouched, he blew out his Achilles tendon trying to fall on a loose ball in the second quarter. Also injured that day were running back Leon Johnson, tight end Eric Green, and nose tackle Jason Ferguson.

Parcells, who had brought in Rick Mirer in the summer, now had to turn to Mirer to replace Testaverde. That didn't go well as the Jets got off to a 1–6 start. Finally, Tuna turned to Ray Lucas, who had his NFL moment in the sun when, executing conservative game plans almost flawlessly, he helped the Jets win six of their last eight. Still, that was only good enough for an 8–8 season.

And the full extent of how that season wore and tore on Parcells became evident the week after it ended, when he announced he was retiring as coach. "You can write it on your chalkboard, fellas," he told another spillover crowd of reporters in the auditorium. One team official, looking for a typical Tuna escape hatch in that message, said, "Hey, chalkboards can be erased." But no, at least as far as Gang Green was concerned, Parcells was done coaching.

First he turned the reins over to Bill Belichick, who, out of equal parts concern about the post-Hess direction of the franchise and Parcells's continued presence, handed the reins back two days later by announcing he was resigning "as H.C. of the N.Y.J," the shorthand he used on his handwritten resignation letter. Then Parcells turned to Al Groh, his long-time linebackers coach, and retreated to his second-floor bunker as the full-time general manager.

The great Tuna schmooze was over. He was most visible that last year when he came out during training camp practices and sat on the top row of the small metal bleachers reserved for invited guests of the team to see how his draft picks and free-agent signings were working out and to trade small talk and baseball riddles with reporters and fans.

One of the last times I spoke with Bill in his role as the shadowy GM was in August of 2000. The situation seems somewhat

The Riddler

Here's one example of a baseball riddle Bill Parcells traded with reporters during the summer of 2000, when he served as the general manager of the Jets: In one inning a team gets two singles, two doubles, and two triples but doesn't score. How is this possible?

Answer: The situation isn't good baseball, but it's possible. The first batter triples but is thrown out at the plate trying to stretch it into a home run. The second batter does the same. With two outs, the third batter doubles. The fourth also doubles, but the runner on second for whatever reason only makes it to third. The fifth batter scratches out an infield hit, with the runners holding. The sixth batter hits a hot smash that strikes the runner running from first to second. (Scoring rule: Single for the batter, but the runner is out and the inning is over with no score.)

surreal, now that I reflect on it. Rain that day had driven the Jets inside their big, white practice bubble for the afternoon camp practice. I was walking, alone, around the back of the two-story complex, across the outdoor half-field, toward the bubble to watch the workout.

Parcells was walking, alone, in the opposite direction.

I was not the closest writer to Parcells—that honor goes to Vinny DiTrani, whom in the eighties Parcells had respectfully

nicknamed "The Sage"—but I had a long history with Bill also. Vinny and I both covered his Giants and Jets teams for *The Record*, his hometown paper going back to his boyhood in Oradell, New Jersey. And shortly after I took over as editor of an independent Giants team newspaper, he told me after his first disastrous season as an NFL head coach in 1983 that he didn't like the way his ghostwritten column in my paper was being handled. I proposed a compilation of his news conference quotes during the season and a monthly sitdown with him during the off-season. He agreed, and that setup worked well until I left the paper early in 1990.

We stopped midway between building and bubble to say hello. As we talked, the black-and-white cat that hung out around the team's field maintenance shed, nicknamed "Tuna" for obvious reasons, walked up and joined the group. Parcells picked the cat up and absentmindedly scratched its head as he talked. "People just don't understand. I can't do this the way I want to anymore," he said. "I could do sixteen games, but I can't do it the way it has to be done. This job takes a lot of energy to do it the way I have to do it."

He was sincere and regretful as he talked, and I believed he meant everything he said. But knowing his track record, I also believed he would resurface someplace else, some other time. "Players play," he has always said, "and coaches coach."

Sure enough, after a year of lying low and getting the juices flowing again, it was as if Roy Hobbs had moved from Iowa to Irving. Parcells struck a deal with Cowboys owner Jerry Jones to resuscitate America's Team.

I'm not the first to say it: Parcells should have stayed, kept it together, and tried to finish the job with the Jets. But it still counts for a lot that Leon Hess landed the Big Tuna for three years and he worked the magic he had to offer to get Gang Green twenty-six minutes away from the Big Dance.

Woebegone Ones, Terrible Twos

Yes, Virginia, draft weekend is like a visit from Santa Claus, with presents for NFL fans everywhere. But the Jets faithful might liken the annual April distribution of college athletes not to Christmas but to Halloween—and insist that over the years, they've been tricked more than treated.

Before getting into the draft sins of the Jets, let's dispel the notion that in plucking fresh talent, the franchise has been no boom, all bust. For instance, Sonny Werblin and Weeb Ewbank got Joe Namath right in the first round in 1965. Legendary Raiders coach and television analyst John Madden once said he couldn't understand how Namath had been left off the NFL's seventy-fifth anniversary team. "Some guys have had a lot of accomplishments," Madden said, "but with Joe, here's a guy who made a league."

Elsewhere in round 1: The year before Namath, Matt Snell was a Super Bowl-winning fullback-to-be. John Riggins began his Hall of Fame career as a Jet in 1971. Sack Exchange anchor Marty Lyons arrived in 1979. Freeman McNeil, who set the franchise rushing records that Curtis Martin has recently broken, came aboard in 1981. Wide receiver Al Toon's brief shining star first rose in 1985. Linebackers Marvin Jones and James Farrior, cornerback Aaron Glenn, and wide receiver Keyshawn Johnson made their marks in the nineties.

Then there's the 2000 draft: a record four first-round picks, all starters a half-decade later with three Pro Bowls to their credit. I'll get to them later.

All that being said . . . Whether fair or not, the perception is that the Jets have always struggled in the draft. At first, in the sixties, it wasn't that important. When first-round picks Tom Brown (1961), Sandy Stephens (1962), and Jerry Stovall (1963) never played a down for the Jets, it was chalked up to lingering ineptitude from the Titans era.

The Jets hit the skids in the seventies, but when Mike Hickey came aboard as the team's player personnel director in 1978, they at least began drafting players such as tackle Chris Ward, Lyons, and Mark Gastineau in 1979, and McNeil and linebacker Bob

Crable in 1981, which set the stage for the team's resurgence in the 1980s.

But many fans don't have fond memories of Hickey. Maybe it was the trade up to get Texas wideout speedster Johnny "Lam" Jones with the second overall pick of the 1980 draft. After a preseason defeat in which Jones fared well, a reporter innocently approached him at his locker after the game and suggested he had a decent game. "Did you look at the scoreboard?" Jones bristled. "We lost the game. How could you say something like that?"

Nice reaction, although extreme for a rookie in his first NFL summer. If only the rest of Jones's career had been so extreme—

Weeb Ewbank with Joe Namath, a number one draft choice the Jets got right. AP

he lasted five NFL seasons, all with the Jets, and his modest 1983 season (43 receptions, 734 yards, 4 touchdowns) was his best.

Hickey's selection of quarterback Ken O'Brien with the twenty-fourth overall pick in 1983 wouldn't have been so heinous, except that he (not to mention four other teams that selected quarterbacks before the Jets) failed to take Dan Marino, who went to the Dolphins at number twenty-seven. With the first-round picks of tackle Mike Haight, fullback Roger Vick, and tackle Dave Cadigan from 1986 to 1988, Hickey cemented his status in many fans' Jets Hall of Shame. He followed that troika up with a "reach" selection of linebacker/end Jeff Lageman in 1989, which generated the following exchange:

> ESPN draft expert Mel Kiper after the Lageman pick: "The Jets have no concept of what the draft is all about."
>
> Hickey several days later: "Are you going to listen to some guy who works out of his basement in Baltimore?"

"Mike thrived on being different," said Rich Cimini, the *New York Daily News*'s tough, long-time Jets beat writer. "He just enjoyed being this maverick, going against the grain. He thought he was smarter than anybody else."

Hickey was replaced in 1990 by new general manager Dick Steinberg, the respected personnel man from New England, who nevertheless got his administration off on the wrong foot by taking Penn State running back Blair Thomas with the second overall pick in 1990. "Dick was the opposite of Mike—modest, down-to-earth," Cimini recalled. "But he had this system based on numerical values. A 6'4", 250-pound linebacker was getting a

The Jets passed on Dan Marino to take Ken O'Brien (below) in the 1983 draft.
Bill Kostroun/AP

high grade. He just put a premium on those measurables. He felt more often than not you'd get a good player, but the Jets ended up whiffing on so many players because of it."

Dick Haley, the well-respected Steelers draft man who brought stability to the process used by the Jets, wasn't involved in drafting Thomas, but he arrived in 1992 to witness the running back's decaying orbit. "My philosophy is not very complicated," Haley said as he drove from a pro-day workout near his semiretirement home in Florida in March 2005. "If a guy is the best player in high school, and he's the best player in college, and he's got the tools, I'm thinking he'll be a real good pro. Blair had a track record, a history. He wasn't just a flash in the pan. He went to a big-time university with big-time players. Why wouldn't he be a good player? Yet some of them are not."

Haley answered his own question by suggesting we follow the money. "We make them rich right away," he said. "When we fill their pockets immediately, suddenly you go down deep into a person's character. If you take tough guys who have dedication, you've got a chance to have good players all the time."

Thomas, despite decent averages (4.3 yards per carry as a Jet, 4.2 for his career), wasn't tough enough. Maybe he couldn't handle being a pro athlete in New York (he wouldn't have been the first). Maybe that key late fumble on the fourth Monday night game of the 1991 season in Chicago, turning a 13–6 Jets win in regulation into a 19–13 Bears win in overtime, signaled the end. Whatever, Thomas's hamstrings were constantly acting up while his offensive touches were going down, and he became an ex-Jet after the 1993 season.

First-rounders make the tabloid back pages, but another measure of an NFL team on the rise or decline is its second-round choices. In theory these selections should all be, if not starters, at least strong contributors for a while. Sure, everyone occasionally misses in this round. After all, the NFL draft is not a science but an art . . . But how to explain the Jets organization's ineptitude in this shriveled slice of their draft past? Until just before the new millennium, they had a fifteen-year run of bad scouting, bad selections, and bad luck trying to come up with decent second picks.

Actually, their difficulties finding a good second banana date to their days as the Titans. From 1961 to 1967, the Titans/Jets had six second-round picks (one was traded away). Of those six only Rutgers center Alex Kroll ever played for the team, and that was for just the 1962 season.

But in the mid-eighties the Jets began mixing their occasional first-round failures with a regular diet of second-round flops. Here is a roll call of the players who have become known collectively over the years as the Jets' "Terrible Twos":

1984—Ron Faurot (1B), DE-DT, Arkansas; Glenn Dennison (2B), TE, Miami (Fla.)

Russell Carter, the first of two first-round picks, didn't set the world on fire, but at least he lasted four seasons. Jim Sweeney was the first of two second-rounders who did yeoman's work, mostly at center, for eleven years. But the Jets second pick that year, which they got from New Orleans in the Richard Todd trade, was Faurot, whose entire NFL career lasted two seasons and twenty games, during which he registered 2 sacks.

The List

Here is a complete list of the first- and second-round draft picks in the Jets history since 1961 (regular college drafts only). *Note:* The 1960 AFL draft was by position, not round. Where there is no pick designated, the selection was traded.

Year	Round 1	Round 2
1961	Tom Brown, G, Minnesota*	Herb Adderley, HB, Michigan State*
1962	Sandy Stephens, QB, Minnesota	Alex Kroll, C, Rutgers
1963	Jerry Stovall, HB, LSU*	—
1964	Matt Snell, FB, Ohio State	Lloyd Voss, T, Nebraska*
1965	a. Joe Namath, QB, Alabama b. Tom Nowatzke, FB, Indiana*	John Huarte, QB, Notre Dame
1966	Bill Yearby, T, Michigan	Sam Ball, T, Kentucky*
1967	Paul Seiler, C-G, Notre Dame	Rich Sheron, TE, Washington State*
1968	Lee White, FB, Weber State	Steve Thompson, DL, Washington
1969	Dave Foley, T, Ohio State	Al Woodall, QB, Duke
1970	Steve Tannen, DB, Florida	Richard Caster, WR, Jackson State

Year	Round 1	Round 2
1971	John Riggins, RB, Kansas	John Mooring, T, Tampa
1972	a. Jerome Barkum, WR-TE, Jackson State b. Mike Taylor, LB, Michigan	—
1973	Burgess Owens, DB, Miami	Robert Woods, T, Tennessee State
1974	Carl Barzilauskas, DT, Indiana	Gordon Browne, T, Boston College
1975	—	Anthony Davis, RB, USC*
1976	Richard Todd, QB, Alabama	Shafer Suggs, DB, Ball State
1977	Marvin Powell, T, USC	Wesley Walker, WR, California
1978	Chris Ward, T, Ohio State	Mark Merrill, LB, Minnesota
1979	Marty Lyons, DL, Alabama	Mark Gastineau, DL, East Central (Oklahoma)
1980	Johnny Jones, WR, Texas	a. Darrol Ray, S, Oklahoma b. Ralph Clayton, RB-WR, Michigan
1981	Freeman McNeil, RB, UCLA	Marion Barber, RB, Minnesota
1982	Bob Crable, LB, Notre Dame	Reggie McElroy, T-G, West Texas State

(continued)

Year	Round 1	Round 2
1983	Ken O'Brien, QB, Cal-Davis	Johnny Hector, RB, Texas A & M
1984	a. Russell Carter, DB, SMU b. Ron Faurot, DL, Arkansas	a. Jim Sweeney, G-C, Pittsburgh b. Glenn Dennison, TE, Miami
1985	Al Toon, WR, Wisconsin	Lester Lyles, S, Virginia
1986	Mike Haight, T-G, Iowa	Doug Williams, T, Texas A & M
1987	Roger Vick, FB, Texas A&M	Alex Gordon, LB, Cincinnati
1988	Dave Cadigan, T-G, USC	Terry Williams, CB, Bethune-Cookman
1989	Jeff Lageman, LB, Virginia	Dennis Byrd, DE, Tulsa
1990	Blair Thomas, RB, Penn State	Reggie Rembert, WR, West Virginia
1991	Rob Moore, WR, Syracuse (supplemental draft)	Browning Nagle, QB, Louisville
1992	Johnny Mitchell, TE, Nebraska	Kurt Barber, LB, USC
1993	Marvin Jones, LB, Florida State	Coleman Rudolph, DL, Georgia Tech
1994	Aaron Glenn, CB, Texas A&M	Ryan Yarborough, WR, Wyoming
1995	a. Kyle Brady, TE, Penn State b. Hugh Douglas, DE, Central State (OH)	Matt O'Dwyer, G-T, Northwestern

Year	Round 1	Round 2
1996	Keyshawn Johnson, WR, USC	Alex Van Dyke, WR, Nevada
1997	James Farrior, LB, Virginia	Rick Terry, DT, North Carolina
1998	—	Dorian Boose, DE, Washington State
1999	—	Randy Thomas, G, Mississippi State
2000	a. Shaun Ellis, DE, Tennesse b. John Abraham, LB, South Carolina c. Chad Pennington, QB, Marshall d. Anthony Becht, TE, West Virginia	—
2001	Santana Moss, WR-KR, Miami	LaMont Jordan, RB, Maryland
2002	Bryan Thomas, DE, Alabama-Birmingham	Jon McGraw, S, Kansas State
2003	Dewayne Robertson, DT, Kentucky	Victor Hobson, LB. Michigan
2004	Jonathan Vilma, LB, Miami	—

* Did not sign with the club.

Running back Blair Thomas flew high at Penn State but landed with a thud as a Jet.
Paul Vathis/AP

And Dennison's claim to fame was that he was born in Beaver Falls, Pennsylvania, and attended Beaver Falls High—exactly like Namath. Dennison's career with the Jets was far from Namathian, though, and shorter than even Faurot's: one season, sixteen games, 16 catches for 141 yards and one touchdown.

1985—Lester Lyles, S, Virginia
Lyles enjoyed a strong sophomore season with 5 interceptions, 4 forced fumbles, and 112 tackles in sixteen games, fourteen of them

starts. Coach Joe Walton even gushed, "If Lester continues to work on all his techniques, he could be one of the outstanding safeties in the NFL." Yet Lyle lasted only three seasons with the Jets, capped by an injury-marred 1987 in which he played four games and had no interceptions. The next year he was in Phoenix.

1986—Doug Williams, T, Texas A & M

A classic bust. Taken forty-ninth overall, Williams had decent tackle size for that era at 6'5" and 286 pounds, and a good pedigree: scholastic ball at Cincinnati's famed Moeller High, second-team All-America at A&M. Yet he never made it out of Jets training camp. He played two seasons for the Oilers before calling it a career.

1987—Alex Gordon, LB, Cincinnati

Gordon began with a bang: 5 sacks as a rookie (which would be his career high) and three seasons with Gang Green before putting in one season with the Raiders and three more with the Bengals.

But so much more was expected from this player with the sculpted 6' 5", 246-pound physique. When the Jets and Giants met for one of their Pennsylvania scrimmages in the 1989 pre-season, Bill Parcells, then coaching the Giants, wandered over during individual drills and said to Gordon point-blank, "How come you're not any better?"

"One time I asked Joe Walton, 'How's Gordon doing?'" Cimini recalled. "Joe's response was, 'Well, he's big,' Damning praise from Walton."

1988—Terry Williams, CB, Bethune-Cookman

Williams was small and powerfully built at 5'11" and 197 pounds. Yet early in 1989 he had yet to make a pro start and had been limited to nickel and special-teams duty. Then he suffered a serious knee injury in game 3 at Miami that required reconstructive surgery, ending his second Jets season—and his NFL career.

1989—Dennis Byrd, DE, Tulsa

Byrd was on his way to becoming a very good if not special player before his devastating injury in 1992.

1990—Reggie Rembert, WR, West Virginia

The first major story about Rembert didn't take long to be written. He got taken for a ride on his way from La Guardia Airport to the Jets' training complex for his first minicamp after the draft. "This taxi driver drove Reggie from the airport all over Long Island," Cimini said. "The guy nailed him for a $150 fare. They gave up on him in training camp and traded him to the Bengals for linebacker Joe Kelly. The cab ride might've been an indication." In his three NFL seasons, all with Cincinnati, Rembert managed a single TD catch.

1991—Browning Nagle, QB, Louisville

Nagle was a double-whammy as a Terrible Two. His career was short and unproductive: three seasons with the Jets, and a starter only in his second season, when he threw for 7 touchdowns and 17 interceptions.

And Nagle had the misfortune to be inextricably linked with Brett Favre. The Jets desperately wanted a quarterback in 1991, and Dick Steinberg and director of player personnel Ron Wolf were well aware of the rough-hewn Favre. But Atlanta, picking directly ahead of the Jets, took Favre, so the Jets were left with Nagle. The next year Wolf became Green Bay's general manager.

First order of business: trade with the Falcons for Favre. The rest, as they say, is history.

Jets fans, meanwhile, still swap Browning anecdotes. One time he called the wrong play in the huddle, so he approached the line of scrimmage with the play clock winding down and apologized to his teammates. Another time, he picked a fight in a Monday night game—with Buffalo defensive end Bruce Smith.

1992—Kurt Barber, LB, Southern California

Another great body at 6' 4", 245 pounds who wasn't cut out for pro-football stardom. Barber lasted four seasons, fifty games, made 3.5 sacks, then succumbed to knee problems. These days he's an assistant college coach in Nevada.

1993—Coleman Rudolph, DE-DT, Georgia Tech

A virtual cipher. "The Jets traded down to get him, but I was stunned when I saw him for the first time," Cimini recalled. "They said he was 6' 4" and 270, but he just looked like a puffed-up high school kid. He was completely out of his league." Rudolph played four games in green, then left for the Giants for three seasons. He had 5 sacks in his pro career, none as a Jet.

1994—Ryan Yarborough, WR, Wyoming

Yes, Yarborough was highly productive on the college level. Unfortunately, that level was the Western Athletic Conference, which has been known to beguile NFL scouting departments with inflated receiving numbers. Yarborough lasted two seasons, twenty-nine games, and had 24 catches with the Jets. He sat out 1996, then went two more with Baltimore.

1995–Hugh Douglas (1B), DE, Central St. (Ohio); Matt O'Dwyer (2), G, Northwestern

These two are the exceptions that prove the rule. Bill Parcells banished Douglas to Philadelphia in a trade, while O'Dwyer left for Cincinnati as a free agent, but both have been decade-long NFL starters.

1996–Alex Van Dyke, WR, Nevada

Like Yarborough, Van Dyke was a product of inflationary Big West receiving numbers. And he was a compound error because while Haley was arguing to take defensive end Tony Brackens at the top of the second round, Rich Kotite inexplicably wanted another receiver to team with Keyshawn Johnson, whom the Jets took first overall. Van Dyke's last vignette as a Jet: dropping a pass late in the 1998 loss to Denver in the AFC title game.

1997–Rick Terry, DT, North Carolina

One thing Parcells and George Young, the late GM, agreed on with the Giants was Young's "Planet Theory": There are only so many athletic big men on this planet, so when you see one, take him. Terry certainly looked the part at 6'4" and 302. Only problem: He wasn't big on pro football. He lasted just his rookie season with the Jets, getting 2 sacks in fourteen games, before he left for Carolina and oblivion.

1998–Dorian Boose, DE, Washington

A friendly, religious young man who was probably too nice to play this game. He'll be remembered for his 2000 season, when he actually started to see action. He was so revved up that in practice he got into a fight with tight end Fred Baxter, who took a swing at Boose's helmet and broke his hand. Baxter was released later that season, Boose in the off-season.

You may have noticed that this litany of woe seems to last forever. Indeed, 1984 to 1998 covers multiple regimes—of draft gurus from Mike Hickey to Dick Steinberg to Haley, and of head coaches from Joe Walton to Bruce Coslet, Pete Carroll, Rich Kotite, and Bill Parcells. That's not a coincidence.

"The Jets have been a little erratic over the years," Haley said. "I've always been with teams where the coaches are involved in the process. When I was with Pittsburgh, we had basically the same people most of the time. When I came to the Jets, it was not that way until Parcells arrived. Whenever you involve your coaches in your selections, you've got to know what they're saying, have a little bit of a track record on them. You find out some guys may be really good coaches but are not great talent evaluators."

Besides a continuity issue, drafting second-rounders is just harder to do than shooting fish in the first-round barrel. "Sometimes we say, 'Okay, we're out of the first round, if we hit with this guy, we've got something really good.' So I think you may reach a little more in that round than you should," Haley said. "I've gone back over a draft and said, 'Here's a guy who wasn't quite as big or fast, but he played every down. We would've been better off taking him than the guy who looked like he had all the tools but that little inconsistency was there. We knew it, we thought we could get over it.' Too often, you can't get over it."

Haley and the Jets turned the corner, with both the Terrible Twos and the Woebegone Ones. The second-round cycle was broken in 1999 with the selection of guard Randy Thomas.

John Abraham (right), one of 2000's "Four Aces," deals a sack to Oakland's Rich Gannon. Julie Jacobson/AP

And what's not to like about the 2000 draft, one of the greatest first rounds in NFL history? Not only did they draft a record four "aces" that year but, with the aid of assistant GM Mike "Mr. T" Tannenbaum, they had them all signed up from the start of their first training camp and all have contributed for half a decade—Shaun Ellis and John Abraham as Pro Bowl defensive ends, Chad Pennington as the franchise quarterback, and Anthony Becht as a starting tight end.

General manager Terry Bradway, who took over in 2001, has had crowd-pleasing first-rounders with Santana Moss (since traded to Washington for 2000 third-rounder Laveranues Coles), Dewayne Robertson, and Jonathan Vilma. "The Jets haven't won the championship yet," said Haley, who passed control of the Jets draft to Jesse Kaye in 2003, "but over the last seven or eight years, we've had pretty good teams. When you have a good coach, then you should be competitive and have a chance to win every year. That's all I've ever asked for."

And maybe after all those tricks of Aprils past, the Jets have finally learned the art of giving their fans and themselves an annual treat at the NFL draft.

Curt's Determined Climb

Curtis Martin is an unimposing 5'11", 210-pounder who, when immaculately coifed and dressed to the nines as he always is away from the field, looks more like a GQ model than the model for the NFL running back. He collects art and still takes care of his mama. He is soft-spoken and thoughtful. The only nickname anyone can come up with for him that sticks is "Curt." The most Sharpie-like thing he's done after scoring a touchdown is to drop the football and give a split-second Incredible Hulk–like pose.

"It's always been about what the team does. That's what matters to me," Martin has said. "All these individual things, I don't even keep up with them. I appreciate them, but they're things I can look back on and read in books after I'm done playing." With that attitude no wonder it took him ten seasons to become the NFL's latest overnight sensation.

But Martin made himself impossible to ignore as he climbed ladders in 2004. Every week, it seemed, he did something else that forced the national sports networks and magazines—the real culprits in his extended pro anonymity—to sit up and take notice.

In the opener, after gearing up all off-season for the fast start that had eluded him recently, Martin slashed past the Bengals for 196 yards on 6.8 yards per carry. Coach Herman Edwards, asked if he'd ever seen Martin run as well, said he had: "My first year [2001], when he ran for 1,500. He has that look about him right now."

In week 2, Martin roared past Freeman McNeil's franchise record of 8,074 career rushing yards. "I had my time. Now it's Curtis's time," McNeil said, with no trace of remorse at the loss of his crown. "We celebrate the things he's doing. Certainly he embodies a work ethic, a commitment to excellence. He brings that to his sport and his team."

In game 6, Martin barged past the iconic and iconoclastic Jim Brown, then number seven on the NFL's all-time rushing list with 12,312 yards. "When you pass Jim Brown," Chris Berman, ESPN anchor and unabashed Jets fan, observed, "you've done something, my friend."

In game 10 at Cleveland, Martin reached 1,000 yards again, the earliest in his career he'd become a grand back, to keep pace with Barry Sanders as the only players in pro football history to rush for 1,000 in each of their first ten seasons. In game 11 at Arizona, he won the "head-to-head" matchup with Emmitt Smith, the NFL's all-time rushing leader, 99 yards to 21.

And in game 16 at St. Louis, Martin worked overtime to become the NFL's oldest rushing champion in the closest rushing title race in league history. He gained 153 yards against the Rams, including 24 in overtime, to finish the season with 1,697 yards—1 yard better than Seattle's Shaun Alexander, who played later that day.

Not a bad tenth year for a player whom not everyone fell in love with when he first arrived on the Gang Green scene in 1998. The problem at first was the price tag—Bill Parcells, who plucked the kid from the mean streets of Pittsburgh in the third round of the 1995 draft and coached him for his first three New England seasons from 1995 to 1997, brought him to the Jets as a restricted free agent with a poison-pill offer sheet that the Patriots didn't want to swallow. But the cost to the Jets was steep—their first- and third-round picks in the 1998 draft to the Pats.

"I was criticized a little bit for spending that much, but I knew more about what I was getting than a lot of other people," Parcells said with his characteristic self-confidence in 2001, two years after leaving the Jets and two years before taking over the Cowboys. "It was unprecedented, though, to give up a one and a three, so I understood it.

"Curtis was still young. I felt like he had for sure five years left, based on the person I knew and his dedication. I don't think there'd be a person now who would say it wasn't worth it. It's one of the best moves I ever made, I know it."

Many Jets fans, and much of the rest of the NFL and the national media, were slow to see it. It's not that Martin wasn't rec-

Curtis Martin made major strides up the NFL's all-time rushing list in 2004.
Bill Kostroun/AP

ognized as a very good back, but he always seemed to be eclipsed by backs more prominent or productive than himself—the Broncos' Terrell Davis and the Falcons' Jamal Anderson, then the Chiefs' Priest Holmes (who beat him out for the 2001 rushing title by 42 yards), then the Ravens' Jamal Lewis, and most recently the Chargers' LaDainian Tomlinson.

Martin had an unexceptional first season in green, averaging a career-low 3.5 yards per carry (limited by knee and thigh injuries that were more serious than he ever let on). He had never been known as a big-play back—even last season, he became the only NFL rushing leader in history not to have at least one run of more than 25 yards. Interestingly, his longest run in his last six seasons was a 56-yard burst off left tackle on a Giants Stadium field white with snow and ice against Pittsburgh in 2003. He was known more for his draws and tosses and cutbacks than for his power running or breakaway speed.

Ian Eagle, who has watched Martin run as a radio sports talk host in New York and a CBS-TV play-by-play announcer, candidly described the problems some had with number 28 on the eve of the 2004 season. "It just seemed that everybody out at Hofstra [University, where the Jets have their training complex] was talking about how fresh he looked, what a big season he was going to have," Eagle said. "My first instinct was, I gotta see it. He's not in that upper tier of backs anymore, that's the perception. And there's no doubt he had heard the same things all of us around the league had heard. I don't want to say I was cynical, but there was guarded optimism because of what we'd seen the last two years on the field."

Martin indeed had heard the chatter that maybe he was on his last legs, had seen the stories that wondered how the Jets might minimize the salary-cap damage by letting him go long before the end of the eight-year contract extension he signed after the 2002 season. Talk about what have you done for us lately. Martin's reaction to it all? "That stuff doesn't bother me," he said. "As tough as you guys are on me, I'm tougher on myself."

If that sounds like a particularly forgiving approach to life's travails, it's no accident. Martin is solidly on God's squad. He doesn't drop hallelujahs into every other sentence like many ath-

Curtis Martin by the Numbers

RUSHING

Year		Att	Yds	Avg	TD
1995	New England	368	1,487	4.0	14
1996	New England	316	1,152	3.6	14
1997	New England	274	1,160	4.2	4
1998	New York Jets	369	1,287	3.5	8
1999	New York Jets	367	1,464	4.0	5
2000	New York Jets	316	1,204	3.8	9
2001	New York Jets	333	1,513	4.5	10
2002	New York Jets	261	1,094	4.2	7
2003	New York Jets	323	1,308	4.0	2
2004	New York Jets	371	1,697	4.6	12
TOTALS		3,298	13,366	4.1	85

RECEIVING

Year		No	Yds	Avg	TD
1995	New England	30	261	8.7	1
1996	New England	46	333	7.2	3
1997	New England	41	296	7.2	1
1998	New York Jets	43	365	8.5	1
1999	New York Jets	45	259	5.8	0
2000	New York Jets	70	508	7.3	2
2001	New York Jets	53	320	6.0	0
2002	New York Jets	49	362	7.4	0
2003	New York Jets	42	262	6.2	0
2004	New York Jets	41	245	6.0	2
TOTALS		460	3,211	7.0	10

letes. "Some of us as players, we overspiritualize things," he said. "I think there's a balance where spirituality plays a role." But he clearly leans on his faith, no harder than he did in 2002.

One high-ankle sprain can keep a player sidelined for weeks, but that year Martin played on two high-ankle sprains—to his left ankle in the season opener at Buffalo and to his right in game 7 against Cleveland. "That season was all about just pushing, pushing myself. It took me to another level in every facet of my life, especially in prayer," he said. "I do believe in praying, but I think I prayed more than I ever prayed that year. With all the pain I had, I had to pray more. I even stopped praying for healing. My mind-set was, 'God, just give me the strength and perseverance to make it through this.'" All the praying, Martin said, "formed some good habits. I always pull the positive out of the negative."

Martin extends his faith to the more secular populations of reporters and fans in a way rarely seen even in the NFL's media- and fan-friendly superstars. He has been observed stepping out of an elevator in the hotel before a road game to give an autograph to an imploring youngster in green.

During one training camp, he was entering the dining hall for lunch when one beat writer asked him if he'd be available afterward for an interview. He said sure, then didn't show. The reporter, used to such slights, moved on to other players. A half hour later, Martin returned and found the writer. "I forgot that I said I'd talk with you," he said. "Do you still need me?" Unheard of.

"Every yard I gain, every point I score," Martin has said, "is a way for me to reach out and touch people."

Even his teammates feel touched. "I've been here for four years, and I learned a lot from Curtis," said LaMont Jordan, who decided in the 2005 unrestricted free agency signing period to become the Oakland Raiders starting tailback rather than getting a smaller raise and continuing to wait to inherit Martin's featured role with the Jets. "Athletically, I've got what it takes to be a big-time running back, but I didn't have the maturity level. I didn't know what this whole thing was about. Now I know. In watching Curt on and off the field, there's consistency, commitment, sacrifice."

"He approaches this game as his life," said quarterback Chad Pennington, who along with Martin had applied the biggest stamps to the West Coast offense of coordinator Paul Hackett from 2002 to 2004, "not as a hobby or as something he does on weekends. He's going to be a Hall of Famer one day because of it." Hackett, who resigned at the end of the season, labels Martin "a phenomenon. I marvel that he's the best player on the field every single day."

And wide receiver Wayne Chrebet calls him a true friend. "I have a rule I call my '1-and-1 Rule,'" Chrebet explained. "You're at exit 1 on the New Jersey Turnpike at one in the morning and you need a ride home. Who's going to really say, 'Yeah, I'll be right there'? He's one of those guys you can count on.

"Probably this offseason, I spent more time with him than ever before, going to Manhattan to grab dinner, going anywhere. He just makes you a better person by being around him. He makes you want to be a better football player, a better everything. He just has that effect on people."

Jim Brown noticed that effect in a pastime that in most ways is far removed from the gridiron: playing chess. Brown, the preeminent Cleveland Browns star of the fifties and sixties, began last year sipping iced teas and playing poolside chess with Martin

Curtis Martin has been the offensive focus since he began wearing green.
Bill Kostroun/AP

Curtis Martin scores a touchdown against the Vikings in 2002. Mark Lennihan/AP

at his picturesque home in the breezy hills above Los Angeles and the Pacific Ocean.

"Curtis is good, and he's always improving," Brown said. "I think he got the best of me the last time we met—he had some new stuff. I'm not technically astute on the various methodologies that have been used by the old masters, but he has a sharp mind and he understands the fundamentals of chess. And he had some definite moves in the endgame that kind of neutralized my movement. Then he closed in for the kill."

"We played six hours, several games," said Martin. "When you play someone like Jim, it's always like chess is a secondary thing. It's become a way for us to communicate."

The two are even working together this year, with Martin joining Brown in his Amer-I-Can organization to assist at-risk youth. Martin wound up at Brown's L.A. home in the first place because his annual quest to find off-season workouts that test his will and optimize his conditioning brought him to southern California. One sun-splashed morning last spring, he found himself staring up at the celebrated Santa Monica stairs. "A friend told me about them and I said, 'Man, I've been looking for some good stairs,'" Martin recalled. "It's just like somebody built them on the side of a mountain. There's something like 220 wood stairs. They're so steep that by the time you get to the top you don't want to come down. I do five sets, up and down, whenever I'm there."

"You might call Curtis an old-schooler. His values are a little different than a lot of young men," Brown said. "The game is commercialized now, these guys are all buffoonery who dance around and get all the attention. The guys who carry themselves with dignity get overlooked. This kid has had a great career. He should be in the Hall of Fame, no doubt about it."

Tony Dorsett agrees with Brown and Pennington about the Hall. The former Cowboys great did not experience any mental whiplash as both Martin and the Steelers' Jerome Bettis passed him and dropped him from fifth to seventh on the NFL's all-time list on the same November Sunday.

"I was impressed with Curtis from the day I saw him on the campus at the University of Pittsburgh, and never has it changed," said Dorsett, a Pitt Panther product like Martin. "He's quite a competitor, obviously. He has a passion for the game and he's quite a gentleman as well."

Martin clearly will have some monster eulogies at his funeral way down the road, but what will it mean five years after he retires, when he first becomes eligible to enter the Pro Football Hall of Fame's Byzantine—some would say archaic—selection process? There will be some resistance to enshrining him in Canton, because his numbers were very good, but not great, and because he's never been the NFL's preeminent back like Brown was in the late fifties and early sixties, Walter Payton and O. J. Simpson in the seventies, Eric Dickerson in the eighties, Sanders and Emmitt Smith in the nineties.

But that would be missing the forest for the trees. Martin plans to play at least two more seasons and probably will look a lot like he did in 2004—although it is hoped for his and the Jets' sakes he won't be seen as much as he was on his career-high 371 carries.

He will demonstrate that great vision and sure cutback ability that has served him so well. He will not put the ball on the turf—his lost-fumble rate is the lowest in NFL history for backs with 1,000 carries. He will continue to provide rock-solid leadership and command respect in the locker room. He will close the 4,989 yards of distance between himself and Smith, who retired after the season at 18,355 yards (although he admits he may retire before he catches Smith).

"Not getting more publicity? It doesn't bother me at all," Martin said. "The way I am, I'd rather people not talk about me. I'm a low-key guy. I realize with the talk, sometimes it's good and sometimes it's bad. I'm not big on that. When it comes, fine. When it's not there, fine."

We'll keep talking about Martin and arguing about his merits and demerits. But Herman Edwards, who labeled Martin the Jets' offensive "bell cow" when he first arrived as head coach in 2001, had a great perspective from which to come to grips with what we can expect from Martin at the age of thirty-two, thirty-three, and older. "Everybody says, 'Why doesn't Curtis get this award, why doesn't he get that award?'" Edwards said. "We're seeing a heck of a football player playing right before our eyes. Just enjoy the show."

Curtis Martin has a style all his own, on and off the football field.
Jennifer Graylock/AP

International Arrival?

Was it coincidence or destiny that general manager Terry Bradway and head coach Herman Edwards took over the Jets' football operations in January 2001, which purists insist was the first month of the new millennium? And that their entrance came a year after Robert Wood "Woody" Johnson completed the purchase of the team from the estate of owner Leon Hess in January 2000, which pragmatists and party animals counter was the real start of the next thousand years?

Either way, something was new about these New York Jets. For starters they were playing a little bigger than they used to, and they were somehow exceeding the boundaries of the metropolitan area, becoming more worldly, in the process.

The first evidence of this was the Jets' response to something out of the evil blue, the terrorist attacks that took down the World Trade Center towers on September 11, 2001. Every American was violated that day, but the Jets were right in the middle of the tragedy. The first week of the NFL's regular season had just concluded, and they and the Giants were the two teams closest to Ground Zero. Members of both organizations had lost or nearly lost friends and family.

And the Jets' next scheduled game was the following Sunday at Oakland. "The last thing we want to do is get on a plane and go to California when all four of those planes that were hijacked were going to California," quarterback Vinny Testaverde said the next day. "My suggestion is if they want to play these games, each owner has to travel with his team to the game."

Testaverde, who actually did construction work on some of Manhattan's skyscrapers as a younger man, was a leading voice on the Jets calling for the NFL to cancel or postpone the coming weekend's games. When commissioner Paul Tagliabue delayed making that decision, a majority of the Jets voted not to play that weekend and to forfeit the game if necessary. And Johnson, the former political fund-raiser, ignored the threat of a $1 million fine from the league if the Jets did forfeit and built a consensus that forced the NFL to move the week-2 games to the week after the regular season was originally scheduled to end in January.

"Our guys were willing to take a stand," Edwards said before leaving for the NFL's 2005 winter meetings in Hawaii. "It was the right thing to do. It was not about playing a game. It was bigger than the game. It was really about paying tribute to all those we had lost, and some silence and some prayer for things that are more important than a sporting event. At the end of the day, our league did the right thing when we shut it down."

Then, in small but significant ways, the Jets tried to help the NFL and the country back on its feet. "I know some of the guys on our team have already made donations of last week's game checks," center Kevin Mawae said then. "Some other plans are in the works, too. A lot of what the Jets are trying to do are long-term things, like scholarships for children of the victims."

And a week after the towers were destroyed, some seventy-five players, coaches, and front-office personnel—even reporters there to cover them—put aside Jet green for Salvation Army red. This battalion spent the day moving case after case of donated soup, juice, and bottled water from the organization's overflowing storage areas, up two concrete stairways from 14th Street in lower Manhattan, to an eighteen-wheeler bound for a New Jersey warehouse.

"We haven't done much. We've only been here a couple of hours," kicker John Hall said. "We just tried to lend a hand to our fellow man. I know I'll be able to sleep a little better tonight."

Sleep didn't come easily when the Jets made their first overseas road trip in team history in the summer of 2003 to play the Tampa Bay Buccaneers, the defending Super Bowl champions, in that year's American Bowl preseason game in Tokyo. Bill Parcells never wanted to endure the headaches and hassles of an American Bowl, and the league has yet to send any of his Cowboys, Jets, Patriots, or Giants teams to a foreign country.

But the Johnson Jets embraced this opportunity to represent the NFL on an international scale—even if things didn't always go smoothly. Edwards, who dares life's inconveniences to ruin his day, looked like one unhappy camper shortly after arrival, as he leaned against the wall of the Chiba Lotte Marines baseball complex, waiting to conduct a short but necessary practice session because the truck hauling the players' equipment got lost somewhere in Chiba Prefecture on the way from the airport.

Jets owner Woody Johnson (right) and the Bucs' Warren Sapp fight for the ball in Japan. Katsumi Katsahara/AP

And the game itself didn't go too well. Even though the Jets forged a bond with their hosts when rookie quarterback Brooks Bollinger hit Japanese rookie wide receiver Yoshi Imoto on a 44-yard post-and-go with less than four minutes to play, they lost the game 30–14, a harbinger, perhaps, of the 6–10 regular season to come.

None of this fazed Johnson, the self-described "fan owner" of the Jets. "When our players look back on their careers, they'll realize this was good," Woody said of the Jets role as goodwill ambassadors. "I think this game is one of those things you just have to do. When you're considered one of the best at whatever you do, more is asked of you. It's one of the prices of being good."

That's the catch, of course. How good have the Jets been? By some measures not nearly good enough to ascend to international status. In three of Edwards's first four seasons as coach, they weren't able to surpass New England in the AFC East, and all the Patriots did those three years was win Super Bowls. The season the Jets did beat out the Pats, 2002, they did it with some providential help from New England on the last Sunday of the regular season, and even then they fell two games short of Super Bowl XXXVII.

"It'd be nice to get another one," said former Jets head coach Walt Michaels, an assistant on their only Super Bowl team in 1968 and still a keen observer of the Jets. "It's getting overdue."

Yet by other measures of the current NFL, and by those of the franchise's own historically rocky road, these Jets are doing well. It's a bottom-line business, and the bottom line is that the Jets have been to the playoffs in three of Edwards's four years, a span of success that only six of the thirty-one other NFL teams from 2001 to 2004 (Houston joined the league in 2002) matched or bettered, and a bounty that has never occurred before in Jets history.

"You look back a little bit at your body of work, and you say all of a sudden these guys have done something," Edwards said. "We've participated in five playoff games. We haven't won 'em all, but we've won a few—that's a good thing. You talk about the [thirty-five regular-season] wins we've accumulated in those four years—that's in the top ten in the NFL.

"You've got to have a body of evidence and try and sell it to the players. We tell a player who comes here, it's not about forty-four years, it's about four years. You can't control the rest of that. You're held accountable for the time you're here. I think the players understand that and take pride in the direction we're headed."

None more so than their franchise quarterback. Chad Pennington has been knocked around the past two years since his Cinderella first season as a starter in 2002, yet that bottom line again tells us that in all his regular-season and postseason starts, he has a 23–15 record—a decent .605 winning percentage—and a remarkable passer rating of 94.6. Those numbers are part of the reason he signed a seven-year, $64 million contract, with $18 million in guaranteed money, on the eve of the 2004 season.

"I feel like we're an organization on the rise," Pennington said in March of 2005 as he pedaled on a recumbent bicycle in the Jets' weight room to get himself in shape, while not jostling his surgically repaired right shoulder. "We are slowly establishing ourselves as a team that can win year in and year out and not just have a flash of brilliance every so often but be consistently good and compete for a championship. You have to earn your stripes, and the way you do that is by competing on that level for a period of time and eventually you break through."

It will take more than Pennington to achieve that breakthrough, of course. Offensively, running back Curtis Martin is still going strong, and new coordinator Mike Heimerdinger has been brought in to improve the output of a passing game that will feature Justin McCareins, his former wideout with the Titans, and Laveranues Coles, who returned to the Jets two years after he departed for the Redskins as a restricted free agent.

Defensively, Donnie Henderson will try to do it better than he did in his sensational debut as a rookie NFL defensive coordinator. He has ends Shaun Ellis and John Abraham and tackle Dewayne Robertson at his disposal. And in the middle of it all is linebacker Jonathan Vilma, who leaped from the University of Miami to make an immediate impact in 2004.

Safety Jon McGraw is clearly one of the believers. "I'm definitely excited about the future," McGraw said. "You look at some of the decisions we made personnelwise last year. Coaching was the difference in our defense last year, and that's only going to get better. There's excitement about the changeup in our offensive schemes, what that's going to bring to the table. Everyone has very high expectations and aspirations."

One reason for such optimism, both inside and outside the team, is not just the quarterback or the head coach but the two together. Their relationship, a focus of some media attention in 2004, is a major influence on the team's fortunes. "Some people view it as a bad thing, they think you're too close to your players," said Edwards, who inherited Pennington from the Bill Parcells–

Al Groh regime, which made him the eighteenth pick in the first round of the 2000 draft. "But the game never changes, and how you communicate with your players is very important.

"You should have a relationship with your quarterback. It doesn't mean you go out to dinner every night, but you've got to be on the same wavelength. Chad's personality and my personality, they fit. It worked out that way when I took the job, when Chad was the backup behind Vinny. The conversations we had went well. We have a bond for each other, a very strong trust in each other."

Coach Herman Edwards and quarterback Chad Pennington are on the same wavelength. Elaine Thompson/AP

Pennington described Edwards as a father figure to him, one of the few father figures he's had in his life. "Needless to say, we have a great relationship. I've always felt if a team is going to be successful, the coach and the quarterback need to be on the same page. I know whatever situation I need to discuss—football, family, whatever—he's there with an open ear. That's always comforting."

Pennington even recalled an instance in 2004 when their closeness paid off. In the Monday night game against Miami at Giants Stadium, the Jets got the ball back at their 30 yard line with 20 seconds left in the first half. So little time was left that offensive coordinator Paul Hackett, Pennington's play-caller for four seasons, left the coaches' box to head down to the locker room and set up for his halftime preparations.

It was up to Chad and Herm.

"That was a situation we had discussed throughout the off-season," Pennington said. "He made it clear to me just to have a play in my head. I went over during a time out and said, 'Coach, I got a play.' He said, 'Run it.' It was just a brief situation where our communication helped win a game. I threw a short pass to Wayne Chrebet, he got it, slid down, and called a time-out. Then we kicked a field goal. To me that kind of broke the Dolphins' back."

You could say that. From a 17–7 halftime lead, the Jets went on to a 41–14 rout of their old rivals.

That was one play Pennington specifically remembered. As for entire games, the still boyish-looking Tennessean said three stood out in his five years as a Jet:

Monday, October 23, 2000–Jets 40, Dolphins 37, overtime, Giants Stadium

The "Monday Night Miracle," the prime-time game that was so exciting it went almost instantaneously to videotape. Actually, the first forty-five minutes were enough to send many television watchers and even a few Jets who weren't at the game to bed early as Miami opened a 30–7 lead.

But Vinny Testaverde reached into his bag of tricks to put up thirty points in the fourth quarter. The game went to overtime when Jumbo Elliott, a tackle in the game as a third tight end, made his first and only career reception from 3 yards out for a touchdown with 42 seconds left in regulation, and John Hall's extra point tied the score. Hall's 40-yard field goal then won it 6:47 into overtime.

Pennington, significantly, puts this game on his short list, even though he was a rookie and didn't play that night. "I remember waving my towel, then coming into the locker room at two in the morning and not being able to talk because my voice was gone," he said. "It was unbelievable. Words can't explain how amazing it was."

Sunday, December 29, 2002–Jets 42, Packers 17, Giants Stadium

This day the Jets needed a lot of help from their friends, and they got it when New England, trailing Miami by 24–13 with three minutes to play, got a touchdown pass and two-point conversion toss from Tom Brady and Adam Vinatieri's 43-yard field goal to tie the game, then won it on Vinatieri's 35-yarder in overtime. Had the Dolphins won the 1:00 P.M. game, they would have taken the AFC East. But their loss left the door open for the Jets, who had opened the season 1–4, to sneak away with the division title if only they could defeat Green Bay at 4:00 P.M.

"Just to feel the crowd enthusiasm, the electricity that went through the Meadowlands that day, that has been unmatched," Pennington said. The game is also on the mental highlight reel of wide receiver Wayne Chrebet, who caught two touchdown passes from Pennington. "That was the best game I've ever played in," Chrebet said. "When the Patriots made that kick, that place was as loud as I've ever heard it. Then we went out and played a team fighting for home-field advantage in the playoffs and beat 'em like it was nothing."

Saturday, January 8, 2005—Jets 20, Chargers 17, overtime, Qualcomm Stadium

The Jets had almost squandered their 5–0 start and a ten-win season by losing three of their last four. But before the end of an overtime loss at St. Louis in their regular-season finale, they knew they had clinched another playoff berth when the Bills lost to the Steelers, and that they would be going back to San Diego, where they had beaten the Chargers 34–28 back in September.

"That playoff win was very gratifying," said Pennington, who had returned to action a month earlier from his rotator cuff tear. "Not too many people gave us a chance. We had ended the season on a bad note, and to be able to go out there and win how we did said a lot about our team. In the locker room that night, there was a feeling of 'Finally, we've shown we can overcome a few odds and still make something happen and be successful.'"

Almost Guaranteed

Jonathan Vilma was a smash hit as the Jets' first-round rookie linebacker from the University of Miami. Vilma stepped in as their starting middle linebacker in week 3 and looked as if he'd been there calling adjustments and making plays for years, earning the NFL's defensive rookie of the year award. He has just the right amount of confidence and humility to endear him to fans and opponents alike.

But being a new member of the franchise that gave NFL fans Joe Namath's guarantee of victory in 1968, is Vilma confident enough to utter a similar pledge? He was asked, as he was shuttling from one interview to another on "radio row" during Super Bowl XXXIX hype week, if he had it in him to guarantee that the Jets would return to the Super Bowl in the near future.

"It's tough to make guarantees. You've got to back them up," Vilma said, tentatively at first. Then his competitive fires kicked in. "I will say we'll be in the playoffs. . . . I want the Super Bowl badly. I can't guarantee it yet. That's a little too tough. But I want the Super Bowl. I will be there."

While many Jets fans reveled in that last game, others, being Gang Green faithful, began to express doubts about Pennington—two years after many of those faithful were anointing him as the second coming of Joe Montana. Pennington has been developing a hard edge to let the second-guessing about his arm strength, durability, and big-game performance roll off his back.

Doug Brien (6) kicked the winning field goal against the Chargers on January 8, 2005. *Mark J. Terrill/AP*

On injuries, for example, he scoffed at those who say that the dislocation/fracture of his left hand in the 2003 preseason and his shoulder injury the next season make him injury prone. "That would be a legitimate argument if it was hamstrings, ankles, shoulder tendinitis, those types of things. You're talking a torn rotator cuff and a dislocated hand, freak things," he said. "I can't control injuries. I can only control how I respond to those injuries and do as much as I can to get back on the field. The last two years I feel I've done an excellent job of getting back on the field for my teammates and beating the medical timelines for my injuries. Now I'm just hoping I can make it through sixteen games injury-free. I'd love to go into the playoffs feeling really good and see where that takes us. That's what I'm excited about."

Yet Edwards knows winning ten games and being eliminated from the playoffs each year won't sustain the excitement. "Are we satisfied?" he says. "No, no, we won't be satisfied until we win the championship." And Edwards, Pennington, all the Jets, and their fans know they won't truly be players on the international stage until they do.